BANTAM BOOKS

TORONTO • NEW YORK • LONDON • SYDNEY • AUCKLAND

ARTILLERY

by
James R. Arnold

THUNDER ONE:

Aerial view of Fire Support Base (FSB) Thunder One, a fixe artillery position on Thunder Road, the heavily contested corridor that ran from Long Binh to Loc Ninh on the Cambodian border. With its concentric defensive perimeter rings and already dug gun pits, FSB Thunder One could be quickly reoccupied as the need arose. The circular design and the cleared treeline assured a 360-degree field of fire.

LONG REACH, LOW ACCURACY:

The M-107 175mm self-propelled gun provided the US artillery in Vietnam with its longest range weapon, capable of shooting a 175-pound shell some 20 miles in a fast, low trajectory. The gun paid for its long reach in accuracy—it was the least precise in US service. The hydraulically operated earth-moving blade on the back allowed it to form its own position. On average an infantry division had one six-gun battery permanently at its disposal.

TUBE CHANGE:

Men of Battery B, 2d Bn, 94th Arty, using an M-5432A wrecker to change the barrel of a 175mm gun. The enormous blast of powder required to launch a shell that weighed as much as a man gave the barrel a short life expectancy; on average one had to be changed after eve 400 rounds.

SPEED SHIFT:

An artilleryman of Battery A, 5th Bn, 42d Arty, levers one o
the two trailing arms of a 155mm howitzer to guide it into a
new position in its pit at FSB Megan. The invention of the
speed shift—a jack beneath the base of the gun that allowe
it to be winched off the ground and swiveled—greatly
reduced both the time and the number of men needed to sh
the gun.

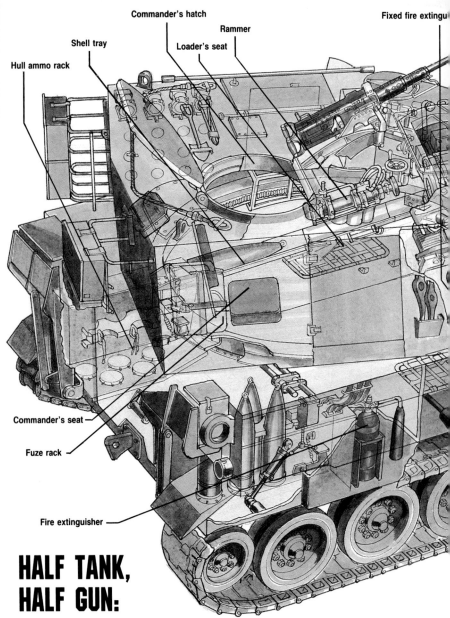

Commander's hatch

Rammer

Fixed fire extingu

Shell tray

Loader's seat

Hull ammo rack

Commander's seat

Fuze rack

Fire extinguisher

HALF TANK, HALF GUN:

The heavily armored M-109 self-propelled gun carried a standard 155mm howitzer tube in an armored chassis wit combat weight of some 23 tons. Apart from its main armament it carried a .50-cal machine gun. With its armo protection and extra firepower it was often deployed in a direct fire role for defending FSB perimeters.

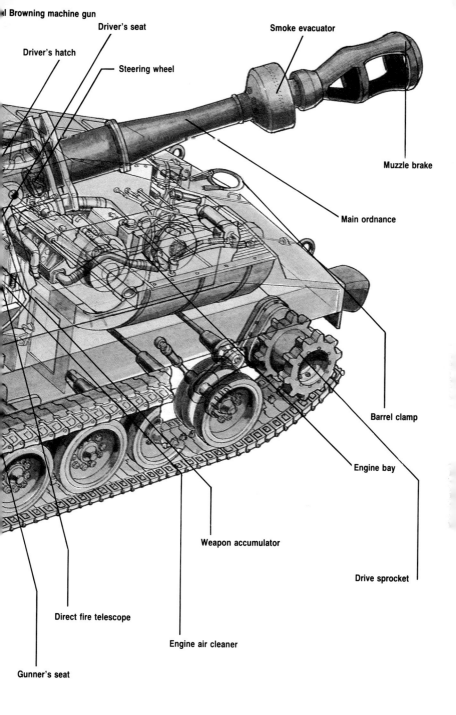

Browning machine gun

Driver's seat

Smoke evacuator

Driver's hatch

Steering wheel

Muzzle brake

Main ordnance

Barrel clamp

Engine bay

Drive sprocket

Weapon accumulator

Direct fire telescope

Engine air cleaner

Gunner's seat

13

EDITORS: Richard Grant, Richard Ballantine. PHOTO RESEARCH: John Moore.
DRAWINGS: John Batchelor. MAPS: Peter Williams. STUDIO: Kim Williams.
PRODUCED BY: The Up & Coming Publishing Company, Bearsville, New York.

ARTILLERY
THE ILLUSTRATED HISTORY OF THE VIETNAM WAR
A Bantam Book/ December 1987

ACKNOWLEDGEMENTS
The author would like to thank the many veterans who took the time to tell
their story: George Allin, Woody Arnold, Dave Campbell, Steve Campbell,
Tom Carter, Larry Caruthers, Willis Crittenberger, Jim Dunn, Jim Gleckler,
Charles Mizell, Mike Vice, Roger Welt.

The photographs for this book were selected from the archives of DAVA,
and the private collection of Woody Arnold.

Library of Congress Cataloging-in-Publication Data

Arnold, James R.
    Artillery.

    1. Vietnamese Conflict, 1961–1975—Artillery opera-
tions.   I. Title.
DS558.9.A77A75   1987   959.704′3   87-26994
ISBN 0-553-34319-X

Published simultaneously in the United States and Canada

PRINTED IN THE UNITED STATES OF AMERICA

CW   0   9   8   7   6   5   4   3   2   1

Contents

The fire adjusters

Forward observers in the field

THE FIVE-MAN Marine reconnaissance patrol, code-named "Primness," strictly followed the four basic rules that they had learned from hard experience: stay together no matter what happens; once in position call artillery fire at a known location, so later fire missions have a reference point to work from; keep in constant radio communication with headquarters; and never stay in one place for more than 12 hours. Rising at dawn, painting their faces and arms with camouflage paint, eating a last hot meal, the patrol boarded a helicopter and departed.

After being deposited in the jungle they climbed toward high ground where they hid and watched. Around noon they heard sounds of someone chopping wood. That night Vietnamese voices and the sounds of movement indicated that the enemy was still around. Primness called in artillery on this target. When the firing stopped there was nothing but silence.

After shifting position at noon of the second day the Marines spotted the first enemy soldier. The patrol concealed themselves and waited. Soon more and more enemy soldiers appeared. Again they called for artillery. This time the guns seemed unable to hit the target. Despite radioing adjustments the patrol could see that the shells kept missing, and missing badly. Then they realized the strong wind was blowing the shells off target. Primness cancelled the fire mission and decided to wait until the still air of the next dawn permitted more accurate firing.

The next dawn, India Battery, 12th Marines received a radio message from "Hateful," the code name for a radio relay station operated by a Marine recon company. Hateful passed on a message from Primness requesting a fire mission. India Battery

commander, Captain Burr Chambless, recognized Primness' call sign. Hateful told him the target was "voices in a stream."

Although puzzled by such a vague request, Chambless ordered his battery to prepare. He knew that recon teams had been specially trained in forward observer missions and didn't ask for artillery without a reason. However, an infantry officer listening in on the radio net decided the request was foolish and inquired sarcastically if "the battery had

The fire adjusters

FIRE MISSION:
A company commander of 1st Battalion, 35th Infantry, calls for artillery in a valley north of Chu Lai. One veteran recalls: "I can't even talk on the radio. . . I'm warbling like a kid going through puberty. You swallow slowly and force yourself to say the coordinates. Everything hits slow motion like you're in your own movie. You try to be cool, calm, and collected and you are. . . kind of. You certainly ain't John Wayne."

time and ammunition to waste on voices in the bushes." Chambless used valuable seconds arguing with this officer before passing the message on to the fire direction center (FDC).

In fact, at this moment the recon patrol could clearly see a worthwhile target. About a dozen enemy soldiers, unmistakably clad in khaki uniforms, were preparing breakfast at their camp along a stream. The patrol's leader had contacted the relay station: "Hateful, this is Primness," he whispered into his

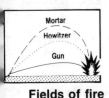

Fields of fire —An artillery piece is described by the height of the trajectory that it normally fires. A mortar shell flies at least as high vertically as it does along the ground. A howitzer round has a moderately high trajectory. A gun fires its shell in a rather flat trajectory.

radio. "Fire Mission. Concentration Papa India five zero niner. Voices in stream bed. One round. Willy Peter. Will adjust."

The men at the FDC had difficulty responding to his request as it came to them from the radio relay station. The target's location was given in code, and the battery didn't know the code's key. A sergeant radioed a nearby infantry unit to obtain the key. This process consumed four minutes. Another minute was spent as the "computers," men trained to calculate and check the technical data needed to fire, worked out the elevation and direction.

An artillery liaison officer then gave the data to an air liaison officer, who ensured that no aircraft were flying in the area where the shells would travel. Until the "Save a Plane" procedure was completed, the fire mission could not begin. While this was going on the artillerymen laid and loaded their guns. They moved without any particular hurry. They did not yet know the nature of the target, thinking that probably some jumpy patrol had been scared by normal jungle sounds.

The fire direction officer plotted the shoot. His map showed that the target was no more than 300 meters from the hidden Marines. Since the patrol was on a hill overlooking the stream, a high-angle shoot would be necessary. Only with the 105mm howitzer tubes pointed almost straight up into the air would the shells pass over the patrol's heads and land in the stream. The officer knew that the night before high winds had blown the shells off target. He worried that an unexpected gust of wind today might drop them down on the Marines.

Finally all calculations, clearances, and safety checks were complete. The battery exec passed on the data to the guns: "Tell the guns the target is talking fish," he joked. The tired, bored gunners appreciated the humor. Talking fish indeed! The recon patrol had clearly been out in the jungle too long, they thought. Eight minutes passed before the first shell fired. No one from battery commander Chambless to the lowest artilleryman felt good about such a long delay.

Forty-eight seconds later the shell exploded off to the recon patrol's right. As the white phosphorous smoke drifted up into the air two VC appeared and casually crossed a bridge just in front of the Marines.

The VC probably thought it was just some more random American firing. The patrol leader whispered to his radioman: "Have them come left one hundred and fire for effect." The battery received the word via Hateful: "Left one hundred—fire one volley for effect." The computers worked quickly, providing the new firing data in under two minutes. Six rounds left the battery.

A grove just across the stream shook with explosions. The patrol saw 15 enemy emerge and quickly ford the water. "Hit them a couple of more volleys," Primness' leader requested. Meanwhile India Battery waited, expecting to hear firing corrections. Instead: "Repeat fire for effect. Eight VC seen crossing stream." Aware by now that they had accurately obtained the range and that the target was an observed, live enemy, the artillerymen responded with zeal. Disturbed from their rest, some 40 VC

Aerial view of a fire support base near the Cambodian border. The guns would be all but useless if it wasn't for the radio network.

surged out from their camp. Although only half-clad, they ran desperately to escape the bombardment. The patrol called for the guns to lay it on thick.

"Left 200, add 100. A platoon of VCs seen running upstream," the battery heard.

Then: "Request area saturation fire. Two hundred VCs moving across stream bed." For 40 minutes the artillerymen loaded and fired as fast as they could.

A last message came: "Cease fire. FO cannot observe. He has been chased off the hill." It was over. India Battery had blasted an area measuring 300

by 400 meters with close to a ton of high explosives. Tired but eager, they waited to hear what they had hit. No further messages came so they went about their business of cleaning their weapons and hauling ammunition. During the day they resumed fire against enemy trackers who followed the recon patrol through the jungle. Their accurate fire discouraged enemy pursuit.

Later India Battery learned that over 50 enemy dead were found on the ground. One artilleryman said: "We were really happy when we heard the results. It made you feel like you were over here doing something."

THE PATROL is walking along a trail. An officer turns to the young second lieutenant, the forward artillery observer (FO). "FO, we need artillery along that ridge." The officer gestures to a distant ridge. The FO sights his binoculars on the ridge and then consults his map. He calls for an artillery marking mission to fire a high explosive shell at the target. In less than a minute the shell bursts on the ridge.

The FO points his compass toward the smoke plume and calls corrections back to the battery. When the marking shots are directly on target he calls the battery to fire for effect, but the fire mission is cancelled. The patrol moves on.

The patrol consists of forward artillery observer students and their instructors. They are engaged in one of the last exercises before completing their training at Fort Sill, Oklahoma, home of the United States Army Artillery School. This exercise is called a "walking shoot," in which the class of second lieutenants is constantly moving while directing fire at different targets. It requires frequent recalculation of the FO's position as well as new fire commands for the artillery battery. In one test the rookie observers have to adjust fire without using a map, or binoculars, or compass. In another they are told they only have four shells to get the job done. In 1969 the "walking shoot" was considered the most realistic and difficult training in the FO program. Compared to the experiences the FOs were about to undergo in Vietnam, the Fort Sills shoot was a cakewalk.

Arriving in Vietnam, FOs appreciated that the first major difference between training and combat was how to adjust artillery fire. At Fort Sill it was done with binoculars and practiced during a course called "Observed Fires." The jungle made it instantly irrelevant. Adjustment by sight in a jungle is impossible. Shell bursts could not be observed and quickly the FOs learned to use their ears as much as their eyes.

With experience, adjusting fire by sound becomes a remarkably reliable technique.

THE US infantry company advances through the jungle in single file. Twenty meters behind the point man, in the middle of the column near the company commander, marches the FO. He is Second Lieutenant Dave Campbell and he follows closely behind

Hill fire —Marines at Con Thien fire a 105mm howitzer at enemy positions in the Demilitarized Zone. One of the standard divisional artillery pieces of the war, the 105mm howitzer, with its short, high trajectory capable of reaching beyond low hills, was especially suited to the conditions in Vietnam. It could fire a projectile weighing around 33 pounds out to a range of 7 miles, 9 with special rocket-assisted shells. Two 105s saw service in Vietnam, the M-101 and the lightweight M-102.

his radioman. When the soldier asks why, Campbell replies: "If a bullet hits you in the chest it has to go through the radio before it hits me." The radioman doesn't quite know what to make of this comment. Campbell is quite serious. The FO is an extremely valuable member of the company.

When they maneuver through a clearing he tries to walk within talking distance of the company commander but some distance away and off to one side. He knows that a hidden enemy sniper who sees three antennas and a collection of nearby soldiers, some of whom are perhaps holding a microphone, will realize he has a command group in his sights. This will be the sniper's prime target. To make it more difficult for the sniper the officers try to stay spread out.

The dense jungle makes heavy going for the company. They stay off the trails to avoid ambushes and booby traps. Progress is slow and the men tire quickly. But this is not the FO's concern. His job is to keep track of the unit's position and to stay in contact with the distant battery of six 105mm howitzers.

Early in his tour the FO had to convince his company commander that he could accurately adjust artillery fire. He'd beg the officer to let him fire a marking round just so he could get the practice. During these first missions he was only allowed to fire a few rounds a day. With experience, and with the arrival of a new company commander, he has more freedom to do what artillerymen love to do: fire the guns.

From in front of the company a burst of small arms fire breaks the stillness. The Americans hit the dirt as someone yells the warning "Sniper!" The lead platoon, some 20 to 30 meters ahead, invisible in the jungle, radios the company commander explaining the situation. The commander turns to Campbell to request a fire mission. Campbell has anticipated the request. As soon as he dove to the earth he radioed the battery "Contact fire mission," gave the location—a six-place map grid designation indicating a point on the ground to within 100 meters—and asked for "Wilson Pickett, 100 hanging." (A white phosphorous shell with a mechanical time fuze was called "Willie Peter" in many units and "Wilson Pickett" in some predominately black units after the soul singer of the mid 1960s.) By the time the

Landmark
—An artillery fire team of the 173d Airborne Brigade fires a special round to mark its 50,000th shell. The unit had been in-country less than one year.

company commander asks for the fire, Campbell's radioman is saying "Shot over." This means the gunners have loaded with white phosphorous, aimed their piece, and sent the shell on its way. With the words "Splash over," the round will explode within five seconds.

The shell detonates in the air, mottling the sky with white smoke above the jungle canopy. Campbell lines up his compass in the direction of the burst. The sound of the explosion comes mostly through his left ear. The aim must be adjusted to the right,

The fire adjusters

FIELD HQ:
Artillerymen coordinate fire support at the field headquarters of 196th Light Infantry Brigade. The rough-and-ready fire direction center has been in action for a while, judging by the air mattress propped on the parapet, but the tangled communications wires on the ground look vulnerable to a careless boot. The Pfc (right) and master sergeant are checking grid coordinates, first stage in the chain of double safety checks between a call for fire and a shell on target.

toward the front of the column and toward the sniper. He radios corrections: "Danger close (the artillery is being asked to fire within 600 meters of the American position), right 200, drop 200, HE on the deck." High explosive (HE) shells will now be fired by two guns of the battery. They are fuzed with a point detonating fuze to explode upon impact.

The platoon leader out front is also adjusting the fire by sound. He radios corrections back to the company commander who informs the FO. The corrections are exactly those Campbell has already

2d Lt. Harold Durham, Jr. —posthumously awarded the Medal of Honor for his gallantry as a forward artillery observer. Although twice wounded by enemy fire, he continued to radio fire adjustments back to his battery. He died with his radio handset still in his hand.

made. Again when the commander speaks the FO's radioman is saying "Splash over." Five seconds later the HE shells explode. The explosion washes over both of Campbell's ears evenly. The shells are on line with the front of the column but still sound too distant. The FO orders the battery to drop another 100 meters. The next explosions sound just right. As the shells fall through their high trajectory and explode just in front of the American positions, most of the resulting fragmentation fans out away from the friendly soldiers. A backwash of pebbles, wood fragments, and an occasional piece of metal pelts the helmets of the front-rank soldiers as they hunker down on the ground. Overhead a large tree limb, severed by a metal fragment, falls to the ground with a crash. This is what close support artillery fire means.

The frontline platoon radios back that the shells are breaking exactly on target. After two more rounds land, the FO tells the guns "End of mission." There is no more sniper fire. In all likelihood the sniper has fled to a concealed bunker. It's hard to hit a single enemy hidden in the jungle with an area weapon like artillery. But the company commander is well satisfied. The sniper failed to hit any of his men and has been driven off. The company has been delayed for 30 minutes but this is not excessive by Vietnam standards. The FO is particularly pleased. For him it has been a picture-book fire mission. The guns were accurate and rapidly on target, before the company commander could even complete his request. The company commander, FO, point platoon leader, and artillery battery have thought and fought as one. Only a little ammunition was expended, seven rounds in all. Best of all, no American lives were lost.

THE COMPANY stands up. Men stretch and flex their limbs. In single file they resume their walk into the vast green bamboo jungle.

At 10:15 in the morning of 17 October 1967, the infantry battalion bumped into the enemy. From concealed bunkers, rifle and machine gun fire flailed the American unit. Second Lieutenant Harold Durham, Jr., reacted with professional cool. He was the forward artillery observer assigned to Battery C, 6th Battalion, 15th Artillery. Durham moved to

an exposed position and radioed firing data to the battery.

When the shells broke over the enemy bunkers, the Communist fire tapered off. During a brief lull, the lieutenant moved through hostile sniper fire to administer emergency first aid to a wounded American.

The sounds of intense combat renewed. Over the radio Durham heard that another American infantry company had lost its FO. This embattled company now faced a powerful enemy infantry assault. Lieutenant Durham moved to join the company and replace the fallen FO. A crippling detonation occurred next to him as he moved. An enemy soldier had blown up a mine when Durham entered the kill zone. Metal fragments nearly blinded him.

Overcoming intense pain, the lieutenant continued toward the sound of the heaviest firing. Finding the company being hard pressed by the

AIRBORNE ARTILLERY

A UH-1B 'Huey' Aerial Rocket Artillery (ARA) aircraft armed with two SS-11 missiles and 2.75 inch rockets. A significant addition to field artillery, aerial artillery was an important innovation of the Vietnam War.

FIRE FOR EFFECT: A 105mm battery of the 101st Airborne Division responding to an infantry call for help. The surrounding hills probably conceal enemy scouts looking for a target.

aggressive enemy, Durham called for artillery fire. In between adjusting the fire, M-16 rifle in hand, he helped the company defend its position. The situation appeared desperate. Durham called for artillery almost directly on his position. The rain of shells twice repulsed the enemy attack.

By now Durham was too weak to stand. Moved to a rear position, the wounded Durham, although weakened by shock and blood loss, continued to adjust the artillery fire. He still refused to seek cover. Instead Durham entered a small clearing where he could more clearly see the fight. As he radioed fur-

ther firing adjustments to the battery, machine gun fire ripped into him. He fell with a second severe wound.

As he lay on the ground the lieutenant spotted two Viet Cong soldiers advancing into the clearing where they began shooting the American wounded. With his last effort Durham shouted a warning. Alerted to the danger, an American soldier shot the two VC. Lieutenant Harold Durham, Jr., 25 years old, died moments later, his hand still grasping the radio handset. He was posthumously awarded the Medal of Honor.

Dien Bien Phu

How not to fight an artillery battle

CARVED DEEP in the minds of every serving US artillery officer in Vietnam was the name Dien Bien Phu. On 7 May 1954, this remote French mountain garrison close to North Vietnam's Laotian border had been overrun by a Communist peasant army. The battle had become a military textbook classic; an example of how a roughshod, underequipped guerrilla army could outmaneuver a well-equipped and well-supplied modern army. The US Army was well aware of Dien Bien Phu. Nobody wanted history to repeat itself; every year on the anniversary of Dien Bien Phu, the guard was doubled at bases and US installations throughout Vietnam.

Artillery had played a decisive role in the battle. From the tops of their bunkers, the officers of the French high command could scan the surrounding green-clad hills. In sharp relief to them were the dusty, open artillery pits of the garrison. In the middle of each pit was a 105mm howitzer positioned so it could quickly rotate to fire in any direction. These howitzers and their accompanying heavy mortars provided the fire support that the French officers believed to be vital to the defense of Dien Bien Phu.

When the visiting French commander inquired about the ability of the garrison's guns to control the nearby hills, he was told by Dien Bien Phu's artillery officer: "My General, no Viet Minh cannon will be able to fire three rounds before being destroyed by my artillery." Reassured, the general decided it was safe to commit more of his forces to the low-lying base.

Back at headquarters French intelligence officers deciphered an enemy message indicating that the Communists were stockpiling an immense amount of artillery ammunition in the hills around Dien

Dien Bien Phu

ARVN ARTILLERY: Vietnamese soldiers hurriedly reposition a 155mm gun to fire against a VC unit that has been flushed by a patrol in 1963. To the horror of US advisers, ARVN guns tended to be widely scattered in small outposts. In the pacification program during the late 1960s, when the US Army faced similar tactical problems, early tactical doctrine went by the board as the Americans too dispersed the guns.

Bien Phu. According to conventional military wisdom a bombardment would have to deliver 50 rounds per hour for each 2.5 acres of target to neutralize the French positions. A staff officer calculated that the enemy could shell the valley with about 33 rounds per minute. The buildup of hostile artillery worried the intelligence officers. When the French commander read this report he penciled in the margin "Why wasn't this study made earlier?"

But it came too late for the defenders at Dien Bien

Phu. The anticolonial Vietnamese forces operating under the Communist banner of the Viet Minh had laboriously carved a supply line through the jungle. Along it they brought the ammunition for the artillery to attack Dien Bien Phu. The payoff came on 13 March 1954. The 351st Heavy Division, an artillery unit structured on the Soviet style, unleashed a ferocious bombardment on the naked French fortifications. The shelling shocked and surprised the defenders; it had been inconceivable to them that the Communists could transport their artillery across roadless mountains and jungles. Nonetheless, the French and African gun crews raced to their weapons and began to return the intense enemy fire. Perspiring in the open sun of the gun pits as they fought back, the gunners took fearful losses. The Viet Minh had carefully plotted each gun's position as well as the headquarters bunkers marked by the tall radio aerials. Here they concentrated their fire. Two French howitzers were quickly eliminated. The French survivors continued to return fire, badly handicapped by not being able to see enemy positions—an essential precondition to the return of accurate artillery fire. Enemy artillery lay concealed in deep bunkers and tunnels hewed into the mountain slopes. Every position was superbly camouflaged. The French forces couldn't see the enemy guns.

To make matters worse the French and African gun crews could not observe the effect of their own fire. On the first day they used up one-quarter of their artillery ammunition. As Dien Bien Phu's officers assessed the first day's combat, the artillery officer's claim that he could silence the Communist weapons rang hollow. It was clear that the enemy

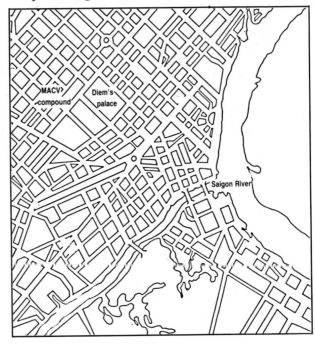

was gaining artillery superiority. In a siege, where the defenders' trenches lay surrounded by the enemy's trenches and there was no chance for maneuver, whoever gained artillery superiority would inevitably triumph. With the first day's hurricane-like bombardment the defenders of Dien Bien Phu began their slow, agonizing death. Although the defenders held on for 56 days, the Viet Minh's artillery superiority proved decisive.

The French lost Indochina when they lost the artillery battle. History had changed, and the movement leading to American military involvement in Indochina had begun.

The French exodus from Vietnam left a vacuum that the United States hustled to fill. American military advisers arrived to help create a new national army that became known as the Army of the Republic of Vietnam (ARVN).

Being an adviser in Vietnam was often a frustrating experience. The initial concern was that the ARVN organization was inadequate to cope with any invasion by regular units from the North. In particular, the ARVN light divisions and territorial regiments lacked artillery support. Consequently, in 1956 the first of a series of major reorganizations began. Notable among the changes was the creation of a 155mm howitzer battalion to provide corps artillery support. ARVN commanders could call upon these big guns to support large-scale offensive operations. By having the guns concentrated in a corps reserve, the high command had access to flexible, heavy fire support. But there was a flip side to this drive to modernize the South Vietnamese Army. As it became increasingly conventional, it became tied to the long logistical tail that accompanies a conventionally configured army. Whether this was an appropriate counter to the enemy's guerrilla light infantry remained to be seen.

By 1960 the reorganization was complete. Each of the seven standard infantry divisions had two artillery battalions; one with 105mm towed artillery and one with 4.2-inch mortars. Critics warned that American advisers had created carbon copies of American infantry divisions. They would be too heavy and too slow. The counter to this criticism was that the infantry—the foot soldiers who would have to win the war—had the same foot mobility as the

Premier Ngo Dinh Diem —South Vietnam's first and longest-serving premier. Appointed in 1954, after years of exile in the United States, he was murdered by his own generals in the coup of 1963.

guerrillas. Under the reorganization the artillery and other support units, with their tractors and trucks, would not participate in field operations and therefore would not slow down the infantry. The artillery would remain behind the front lines, secure in the rear areas.

As experience revealed, this line of reasoning was wrong. Since Vietnam had no completely secure rear areas, all logistical units required security forces. Soldiers manning guard posts along highways and at bridges in order to ensure the flow of supplies to the artillery bases, as well as those dug in behind defensive perimeters to protect the warehouses, garages, and repair facilities necessary for a conventional army, were just as surely dropped from com-

bat operations as if they had been hit by enemy bullets.

Furthermore, although the South Vietnamese Army was patterned on American models, it had much less artillery support. An American division had seventy 4.2-inch mortars and 105mm howitzers as well as 12 of the larger 155mm pieces. The newly reconstructed ARVN division had only 24 mortars and 105mm howitzers. By adding conventional logistical support the division sacrificed mobility. Yet it couldn't call upon nearly as much fire support as an American unit. The result of this unhappy compromise was the creation of a roadbound army reluctant to maneuver beyond support range of their artillery and lacking the overwhelming

BUILT TO LAST: In contrast to temporary bases, this ARVN fire support base, headquarters of the 2nd Regiment at Camp Carroll, shows the orderliness of a permanent fortification. The strongly constructed parapets around each gun position have two roles: first, to contain the effects of explosions, whether accidental or caused by enemy artillery; second, to allow for protection against small arms fire in the event of infantry attack. Bunkers at each position contain powder and projectile stores.

Well-advised —ARVN Special Force strikers, working with a senior US adviser, fire a 60mm mortar against an attacking Viet Cong force. Elite troops like these responded well to US training.

firepower that could destroy the enemy when combat began.

In the early 1960s, before the arrival of regular American combat troops, the shortcomings of the ARVN forces—including the weakness of their artillery—seemed so crippling that it was only a matter of time before the country fell to the Communist guerrillas.

Most aware of these shortcomings were the American military advisers, faced with the difficult and dangerous job of turning the ARVN into an effective fighting force. One adviser's lament well expressed the frustration experienced by American officers assigned to South Vietnamese units:

> *I can't pull the throttle,*
> *I can't ring the bell,*
> *But if this goddamn train should stop,*
> *I'm the one that catches hell.*

The problems were deep-rooted: the US advisers worked with an army whose soldiers had a completely different set of values; effective communication was difficult, with few advisers capable of speaking Vietnamese.

American advisers had one-year tours of duty. With the can-do American spirit, they felt anything could be accomplished with hard work during that year. South Vietnamese soldiers who had fought the enemy all their lives didn't understand why the advisers thought the war could be won overnight.

The sharp contrast in experience and attitudes showed up all the time. The senior American artillery adviser in the vital Military Region IV, the populous delta area south of Saigon, was a young, inexperienced lieutenant who arrived for his first tour of duty in Vietnam in 1971. His South Vietnamese counterpart was a Colonel Phuc, who commanded the corps artillery in the region. Phuc had 19 years of combat experience. He had been a member of the first Vietnamese artillery battalion that the French had organized to aid them in their fight against the Viet Minh. When South Vietnam became an independent country, Phuc went on to command its first artillery unit. He was his country's version of Henry Knox, George Washington's great artilleryman in the American

HIGH GROUND: ARVN artillery above An Khe Pass on Route 19 in the Central Highlands, one of the many sections of highway known to Americans as "Ambush Alley." During major operations in a particular region, chains of fire bases would be set up along supply routes to provide fire support for the supply convoys that faced almost daily attacks.

Revolution. Yet, with such vast experience, the colonel had to listen to a young, green American lieutenant tell him what should be done. Furthermore, it was the 24th American adviser Colonel Phuc had worked with.

From the adviser's standpoint Phuc was "quite

PERIMETER DEFENSE: Rows of *abatis*— sharpened stakes—provide perimeter defense for a MACV and Popular Force compound at Binh Tri.

competent and the only problem is overcoming lethargy and helping him get other people to do what he desires to have done." Perhaps the adviser confused "lethargy" with combat fatigue. History does not record what the Colonel thought about his adviser.

Advisers were supposed to do nothing more than advise and suggest. Yet they were judged on how well the ARVN unit they worked with performed.

Sometimes the inability to communicate reached critical proportions. One artillery adviser to an ARVN battery heard over the radio net that a nearby American unit was fighting for its life. The

adviser went to the fire direction center and provided firing data to the battery. The battery refused to fire, claiming that South Vietnamese soldiers were on the ground in the target area. The adviser threatened to kill the South Vietnamese battery commander. The South Vietnamese commander relented and the battery delivered effective fire for several hours.

Then the battery commander informed the adviser that he was running low on ammunition. If the battery shot more than a certain amount of ammunition, the ARVN commander had to pay for the ammunition from his own pocket. Fortunately the

Lt. Brian Thacker —celebrating in Honolulu on his way to the White House to receive his Medal of Honor. It was awarded for his courage in calling friendly fire on his own position in order to give his men a chance to escape.

adviser was able to arrange for a resupply mission with headquarters. The battery's fire helped defeat a major enemy assault.

But there were artillery advisers who became close to their South Vietnamese counterparts. The South Vietnamese returned this affection and loyalty. A battle late in the war on a remote hilltop along the Laotian border highlights the adviser's dedication.

Just as they had been the first to take to the field in Vietnam, so the American advisers were among the last to leave as American combat forces went home. Twenty-six-year-old Lieutenant Brian Thacker served in the field artillery. Recent combat experience had shown that South Vietnamese forces all too often still lacked the ability to effectively employ their artillery. As part of Vietnamization, Thacker's job was to try to train ARVN artillerymen how to fight to hold their country once all Americans were gone.

Officially the lieutenant was team leader of an integrated observation system assigned to two small ARVN units at a fire base in Kontum Province. Kontum lay hard against the enemy-dominated Laotian border. The North Vietnamese could strike at any time. When they did, Thacker's "official" role as teacher and adviser disappeared.

At dawn on 31 March 1971, an overwhelming enemy force assaulted the small, isolated hilltop fort. Elite sappers spearheaded the attack using flamethrowers and explosive charges to break through the fort's protective wire. A devastating barrage of rockets and grenades kept the defenders pinned to their bunkers as the North Vietnamese entered the fort. Thacker rallied the defenders, including a handful of American soldiers, and led them from their bunkers to confront the enemy soldiers in hand-to-hand combat. When not leading charges, the lieutenant operated an exposed observation post from which he directed Allied aircraft and friendly artillery fire against the attackers. In spite of intense automatic weapons fire directed against his post, Thacker persisted for four hours. His bravery allowed the fort to hold into the afternoon.

By late afternoon it became clear that the fort was about to be overwhelmed. Lieutenant Thacker organized an escape, rallying the tired defenders and

giving them a will to live. Thacker fought a one-man rear-guard action as he covered the fleeing Allied forces with fire from his M-16 rifle.

According to the words on his citation: "In an act of supreme courage, he called for friendly artillery fire on his own position to allow his comrades more time to withdraw safely." Thacker fell, so badly wounded that he couldn't escape with his men. He managed to crawl to a hiding place and amazingly evaded detection for seven days. On the eighth day friendly forces recaptured the fort and found Thacker still alive.

In the words of his commendation: "The extraordinary courage and selflessness displayed by Lieutenant Thacker were an inspiration to his comrades and are in the highest tradition of the military service." Lieutenant Brian Thacker, Field Artillery, Battery A, 1st Battalion, 92nd Artillery, received the Medal of Honor for his gallant conduct.

WHEN THEY WERE properly led and equipped, South Vietnamese soldiers fought as well as any

Dien Bien Phu

SELF-CONTAINED: Members of the 3d Bn, 219 Arty, attached to the 173d Airborne Brigade, load a 105mm howitzer during a fire mission. Artillery and infantry have always had close ties, but nowhere was this more true than in Vietnam where they were frequently isolated together in hostile terrain. Each depended on the other for survival—the artillery needed infantry for base protection, the infantry needed artillery for fire support in the field. To foster the closest possible cooperation, units were kept together, often entering and leaving the country at the same time.

soldiers in the world. The advisers contributed great-ly to their performance. But the rapidly expanding ARVN military could not absorb the sudden influx of men and material. After the Tet Offensive in 1968, fifteen entirely new artillery battalions entered the Army. When Vietnamization, the pro-cess of handing the war back over to the South Viet-namese as the Americans withdrew, came into full swing, the ARVN artillery grew from 29 battalions in 1968 to 58 in 1972.

The transition from relying on American firepower and technical expertise to having to do it themselves proved too much for the ARVN artillery. They fought well, but too few had received the training necessary to handle the sophisticated weaponry of a modern army. This lack of training plus severe ammunition shortages, caused by the American decision to shut off the supply tap once American soldiers departed from the war, contributed to the eventual defeat of the South Vietnamese Army.

LZ Lima Zulu

Air Cav in the Central Highlands

THE FIVE HUEYS touched down on the red clay trail running along a naked ridgetop. The air cavalrymen quickly fanned out in a circle to secure the landing site. With a shout three troopers fell from sight, accompanied by the sound of crushing foliage. The three had fallen into concealed punji pits, which had sides lethally lined with sharpened bamboo stakes. But instead of spearing the troopers, impaling their feet, the brittle punji sticks broke. Sheepishly the troopers stood up and continued. Within minutes Landing Zone (LZ) Lima Zulu had been secured. The cavalrymen waited for the artillery to arrive.

At four o'clock that afternoon Captain Don Whalen, commander of Bravo Battery, 2d Battalion, 30th Artillery, received orders to move his men immediately to a distant clearing where he would set up his guns to support a cavalry force operating in an adjacent valley. Whalen alerted his men and took off for a quick helicopter reconnaissance. He judged his assigned position too small to hold his battery. A nearby peak seemed better, so Whalen chose it for Bravo Battery's position. In the general haste no one took the time to name the landing zone. It received the redundant name LZ Lima Zulu.

In the rush to complete the move before nightfall, no one realized that a friendly South Vietnamese battalion was operating just outside the landing zone. It was a typical Vietnam situation with the artillery just as much in the front line as the infantry, a marked contrast to previous wars where the artillery had trailed the infantry into battle, providing fire support from a location somewhere in the rear of the main battle line. Whether horses pulled the guns or the guns were mechanized, the tactical procedure was the same: find a position combining

Fire Support Base Bastogne, west of Hue. Crowded hilltop artillery positions like this provided tempting targets for enemy mortar and rocket attacks. The importance of this particular base is shown by the quantity of radio aerials.

good observation of the enemy and good security from enemy action. By World War II with guns capable of ranges measured in miles, this invariably meant a position well out of the front line.

Vietnam was different, a war without fixed lines. To meet this challenge the Army created a new type of unit; a completely airmobile division that used helicopters to maneuver. Such a unit could not rely upon conventional roadbound artillery support. If the men moved by helicopter, then the artillery would have to travel that way as well. Accordingly the 1st Air Cavalry Division invented new artillery tactics. But in 1966, early in the war, they were still largely untried.

So it was that the big Chinook helicopters delivered Bravo Battery to LZ Lima Zulu. Four choppers made 13 trips to move the entire battery: men,

cannon, and 860 rounds of ammunition. The first
Chinook set down the battery commander's jeep and
command trailer. The second brought in an advance
party of artillerymen who received the third chopper carrying the disassembled gun and a sling full
of ammunition. Immediately the crew assembled the
gun so it could begin to fire registration shots in support of a distant Air Cav battalion.

The registration shots gave the battery a reference
point so it could accurately conduct future fire missions. Spotters radioed back corrections for these
registration shots. The gunners made appropriate
range and direction adjustments. Five minutes after
the arrival of the first Chinook, part of the battery
fired in support of the ground operations. Unfortunately, the noise of the helicopters and the roar
of the guns drowned out the sounds of the nearby

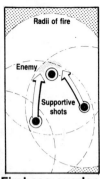

Firebase overlap —The enemy habit of "hugging" close to US units meant that when a firebase came under attack the enemy could often only be hit from a neighboring base, particularly if the enemy was making full use of folds in the ground, ravines, and so on. Every effort was made to place new firebases within range of already existing ones.

ARVN battalion, which was fighting for its life just 600 meters away over the next ridge.

Finally, around six o'clock, Bravo Battery's infantry support, Alpha Company, of the 2d Battalion, 502d Infantry, 1st Air Cavalry Division, received an urgent radio message from the embattled ARVN unit: "We are under heavy mortar attack. . . . They are so close to us that we can hear the rounds going down the tubes." In spite of this call somehow the message was either not delivered to Bravo Battery or its import was not appreciated. Bravo Battery continued to fire to the north, in the opposite direction of the ARVN unit. In the haste to move the battery into position, a remarkable feat of airmobility, nobody had established that the battery had landed right next door to a major firefight.

Hostile fire started to spatter the air as the last Chinook flights hovered over LZ Lima Zulu delivering M-102 105mm howitzers, new lightweight guns specially designed for airborne artillery. No one knew where the enemy fire was coming from. The last guns were delivered and the entire six-gun battery was now in position. As the artillerymen began to dig in, Alpha Company sent out a small patrol toward the ARVN unit. Heavy enemy fire quickly stopped its advance. With nightfall coming fast—in these latitudes dusk did not last long before full darkness came—the cavalry pulled back to a defensive perimeter around Bravo Battery. Outlying patrols continued to bump into the Viet Cong throughout the night. For the artillerymen the first night proved uneventful. At first light they wakened to finally deliver 36 rounds in support of the ARVN unit. They blasted the nose of the ridgetop separating them from the ARVN position. Whether they hit anything no one knew.

During the day cavalry foot patrols searched for the elusive enemy along the ridgetops and in the valley below Bravo Battery. In the afternoon Whalen's men received a request to support a battalion in contact with the enemy. Fifty accurately delivered rounds allowed the cavalry to press on. Moving into the cratered area where the shells had fallen, the cavalry became dispersed. Enemy fire suddenly erupted from all sides. After a confused hour of shooting, the cavalry radioed for more artillery. This time they asked Bravo Battery to split

AMMO DROP:
A CH-47 "Chinook" prepares to drop a load of 105mm ammunition to a battery of the 29th Artillery in Kontum Province. Without fuzes, shells could be treated extremely roughly, with no danger at all.

its fire to cover two separate American groups. Two different azimuths (the compass directions necessary to point the guns in the correct direction) were given but something went wrong. Three guns dropped their rounds just where they were needed, the other three shelled their own men, killing five and wounding five more.

Back on the ridge, ignorant of this awful drama, the battery settled in for its second night. Captain Whalen felt particularly tense. He warned his

LZ Lima Zulu

BIG LIFT: An Army CH-54 "Sky Crane" carries a 105mm howitzer to 101st Airborne Division units fighting in Kontum Province. The M-102 was a light load for the Sky Crane, which could heft a 155mm gun, but ammunition supply by air was a problem for the bigger caliber weapons. The giant chopper's cockpit has windows all around so that the crew can observe their load.

executive officer: "We're a mighty good target tonight; make sure of our noise-and-light discipline." Unfortunately these precautions were not coordinated with the cavalry who manned the defensive perimeter. Alpha Company and Bravo Battery would act independently of one another.

Two hours after midnight exploding mortar rounds woke the captain. Since his own guns were silent Whalen could distinctly hear 21 rounds strike the battery's position as he quickly dressed. Stepping from his tent he saw the gun crews—many barefoot and half-dressed—rising from their pup tents and running to their guns. Beyond them,

rushing straight at gun Number Six, was a massed enemy infantry charge.

Most of the cavalry assigned to defend the battery were either out on patrol or facing the wrong way. Only one platoon remained in direct support. It opened fire with machine guns and M-16 rifles. Some 40 North Vietnamese avoided the bullets. Throwing grenades and firing their rifles, they ran in against gun Number Six. An American sergeant, standing next to the gun, staggered backwards and fell dead when a grenade detonated at his feet. A corporal, hit by another grenade, was blown into a foxhole where he fell on an artilleryman, who then dragged the corporal back to the relative safety of gun Number Three while the rest of gun Six's crew fled from the position. Having overrun the gun, the NVA infantry dropped to the ground and continued to fire at the battery. A second enemy group tried to overrun the battery's nearby vehicle park. A six-man outpost stood in their way. The outpost made a game fight, but had to fall back. The enemy soldiers began to loot the battery's vehicles.

Ten minutes into the firefight, Captain Whalen stood at his fire direction center (FDC) and tried to summon help on the radio. A barrage of mortar shells destroyed the FDC while shrapnel hit the fire direction officer and the soldier who computed firing data. So far none of Bravo's big guns had been fired. Captain Whalen still didn't know all the locations of the friendly troopers assigned to protect his battery.

With his FDC destroyed, the captain yelled to a nearby artilleryman: "Put that PRC-25 (a portable radio) on your back, follow me, stay right with me, don't lose me for a second!" The soldier did exactly as he was told, becoming one of the heroes of the night. Back into the fray the two went. Whalen radioed an artillery operations officer at a nearby camp, explained his situation, and asked for help. That officer promised that ARVN artillery would soon fire to support Bravo Battery. Whalen decided to order his own pieces into action even though he still didn't know where all the friendly troops were. If nothing else, he reckoned, the activity of firing the guns would calm the gunners and restore their

JUST LANDED: Gun crews of the 2/7th Artillery, 1 Air Cav (Airmobile) setting up a firebase. A 105mm gun, its crew, and a load of ammunition made up a single load for a Chinook, the first to be delivered to a new firebase when the Air Cav was on the move.

morale from the shock of the surprise enemy assault.

But before the gunners could act the NVA infantry rose up and charged Number Three gun. Again a shower of grenades heralded the assault. The wounded American corporal who had been dragged from Number Six gun tried to evade a grenade and was hit instead by a bullet in the heart. A grenade fragment struck Whalen's wrist while other pieces of shrapnel seriously wounded five other artillerymen. The gunners resorted to infantry weapons, firing M-16 rifles to save the position. At a range of only a few feet their fire halted the NVA.

Overhead an American airplane, of the type known to all soldiers as "Smokey the Bear," arrived to drop flares to illuminate the position. Undaunted, the brave NVA soldiers attacked again. This time, according to an artilleryman, it "was like shooting fish in a barrel." The enemy stood in bold relief under the flare light. Whalen fired a rifle clip on full automatic and saw three men fall as the charge collapsed.

Whalen led his men back to gun Number Six, and found it damaged beyond repair and surrounded by dead and dying enemy soldiers. Simultaneously the ARVN artillery began to fire, although their shells dropped too far away to provide any real help. Over the radio he heard that an American battery of 155mm guns was moving to get into position to help. During a lull some Hueys landed to fly away the badly wounded. Here was the American war machine running on all cylinders; friendly artillery rapidly responding to a cry for help, an airplane turning the concealing shadows of the night into revealing outlines, choppers landing to rescue the wounded.

Surprisingly, shortly before dawn at just after 0400 hours the enemy tried again. By now Whalen had established where all the friendly troops were, and ordered his guns into action: "Turn those guns around and let them have it," he shouted to the crews of Numbers Three and Five. At the impossibly short ranges of 25 meters the guns blasted the enemy from the ground around Number Six gun. They lifted their fire to smash the enemy riflemen struggling through the bamboo in a last desperate effort to attack.

The assault broke and the enemy tried to flee. They

Alert sentries sandbagged bunkers and cyclone fencing (to stop rocket-propelled grenades) to protect Firebase Tomahawk in September 1969. Enemy sappers could get through the most sophisticated defenses, in the toughest terrain. In June the same year four boys from the same small town, Bardstown, Kentucky, were killed in a VC attack on Tomahawk.

AFTER THE BATTLE: A 155mm howitzer knocked out in a night attack on a firebase near Kontum is inspected at dawn by men of the defending infantry company, A Company, 1/35 Infantry.

had to run a gauntlet of American fire as the repositioned 155mm battery opened fire while a C-47 airplane mounted with three miniguns—modern versions of the Gatling gun capable of firing 5,400 rounds per minute—saturated the enemy with a deadly rain of lead. Finally helicopter gunships followed by fighter bombers carrying napalm bombarded the fleeing foe. Bravo Battery added its own 105mm shells to this inferno of fire. NVA soldiers fell by the tens.

So the surprise enemy attack against Bravo Battery ended. When the attack began the NVA had everything in their favor. They had thoroughly scouted the American position and attacked from an unexpected direction. Their attack began with the

artillerymen asleep in their tents. Their mortars
knocked out the American command center in the
first minutes of the fight. Command confusion on the
American side prevented the defenders from using
Bravo's guns directly against the charging enemy.

Fighting as foot soldiers Bravo Battery recovered
from the shock and stopped the first enemy surge.
They held on until the formidable American arsenal
got organized and delivered a crushing defeat on the
attackers. For all the high-tech equipment and new
tactics of the Air Cavalry, it had been an old-
fashioned, point-blank duel between brave soldiers
using rifles and grenades. In the end the determination of the gunners to keep their battery from being
overrun won the day.

Call in the artillery

The tactics emerge

THE FIRST SERIES of firefights between North Vietnamese regulars and American soldiers provided salutary lessons for both sides.

Led by General Vo Nguyen Giap, the architect of victory at Dien Bien Phu, the Communists concluded that they would have to strike hard and fast when engaging the Americans. They would then quickly withdraw before the vast arsenal of US firepower could be deployed against them.

Their infantry would try to fight at extremely close range and get inside the American artillery umbrella. This, they reasoned, would make the Americans reluctant to call for artillery since the enemy was so close that any slight error would cause the artillery to hit friendly troops. Unwittingly or not, by adopting these close-range tactics, the NVA/VC forces copied German tactics of World War II. The Germans had also confronted American infantry supported by overwhelming artillery. They too had tried to fight right up against the American lines in order to avoid its crushing fire. Over 20 years later a new enemy was using an old tactic.

The other tactic used by VC/NVA forces to counteract American artillery fire was, whenever possible, to mingle with civilians or establish positions in areas they knew the Americans would be reluctant to fire against.

Religious shrines and temples or densely populated areas were favorite sanctuaries. If the Americans went ahead and shelled the targets and killed civilians, the Communists claimed it as an example of barbaric American behavior. It was a tactic designed to make good headlines in the world press and recruit antagonized locals to their ranks. If the Americans didn't fire, the VC/NVA forces had

Main jungle areas of South Vietnam where the tree canopy was thickest.

61

Screamers —Scraps of metal or razor blades inserted between the fuze and shell body produced a high-pitched screech as the round spun out of the barrel at near supersonic speed. An unofficial practice, "screamers" were justified by the gunners on the dubious grounds that the sound frightened the enemy. However, the gunners' officers reckoned the enemy would take comfort in the inevitable adverse effect screamers had on accuracy.

effectively neutralized a major American weapon.

A platoon leader in the Air Cav recalls leading a surprise attack against an enemy-held valley, where the NVA had forcibly employed Montagnard laborers to grow crops to supply their soldiers. When the cavalry suddenly appeared the NVA tried to attack. They forced the Montagnards across the fields along with them, thus sheltering themselves from the American fire. Only when they approached within 100 meters of the cavalry position did the soldiers separate from the civilians. The platoon called for artillery help. Accurate fire shattered the enemy attack. It had been a hair-raising experience and one that narrowly avoided tragedy.

The speed of the American artillery response was staggering. Thirty-six rounds from a 105mm battery could be in the air heading for the target before the first shell even landed. When American coordination went smoothly, an enemy sniper could find himself under bombardment in less than two minutes from the time he opened fire. Batteries constantly worked to reduce their response time. They knew that the initial minutes of a firefight were crucial. As one FO reported: "Receiving fire support in just a few minutes is impressive. But when you are ambushed by an enemy who is firing from hidden positions that surround your men, 60 seconds goes by very slowly."

The time it took for the artillery to fire could be effectively reduced by keeping the battery on standby. If the FO or unit commander anticipated enemy contact, he could radio the battery to be ready. Furthermore, if he could provide the map grid where the engagement would probably take place, the artillerymen could precalculate the firing data and thus be ready for instant support. Since the time for the shells to travel to a target ranged from 20 to 55 seconds for the 105mm battery (it depended on the range and the angle of fire), and firing corrections went very fast, shells could be breaking on the enemy position in very short order.

On the flip side, a battery that was not on standby and suddenly received a fire request at a new, unknown location could use up vital minutes before opening fire. The men might be asleep in their pup tents or part of the crew might be detailed to routine assignments such as filling sandbags or preparing food. Valuable time would be lost while the crew scrambled to their guns. More time would be spent computing the firing data. Safety clearances would have to be obtained from headquarters. Sometimes the entire procedure took a maddeningly long time.

There was also the jungle factor. The overhead canopy of dense foliage not only helped to to conceal the enemy and make artillery observation difficult, if not impossible, but also protected the enemy from the full explosive power of the shells. In open terrain the lethal zone for an exploding shell ranged from a 30-meter diameter for a 105mm shell up to a 75-meter circle for an 8-inch shell. Thick vegetation severely reduced these blast circles. In the thick of the jungle where so many fights took place, the shells had to descend through a triple canopy of thick vegetation. The trees both deflected the shells and caused them to explode prematurely before they reached the ground.

Artillerymen spent many evenings in Vietnam talking shop about how best to penetrate the jungle canopy, which physically shielded the enemy from the full wrath of their guns. Setting the shell's fuze on delay helped. The delay slowed the time until the shell exploded, increasing its chances of reaching the ground. An alternative, in theory at least, was to use one salvo of shells to tear holes in the jungle canopy, permitting subsequent shells to reach the ground.

This use of artillery as a key element in counter-insurgency warfare was a singularly American innovation. It was not uncommon in Vietnam to have an entire battery fire to suppress one sniper. The doctrine of firepower superiority was frequently translated into overwhelming firepower.

Changes in the type of combat bred innovation and invention. None was more marked than the artillery's ability to fire in a complete 360-degree circle. Previously, when artillerymen trained at Fort Sill they used fire fans aimed forward that covered up to 90 degrees. Suddenly, plunged into a war in Vietnam with no front lines, they had to respond in all directions. This required both a different way to think and some new tools to get the job done.

The textbook method of changing the firing position of the large 155mm towed howitzers was both time-consuming and physically draining. In order

The white phosphorus shell—known as WP or Willy Pete—used as an incendiary or for a sighting shot in jungle terrain was a modification of a standard chemical shell. The high explosive was confined to a tube running down the center of the shell, surrounded by the white phosphorus mixture. The bursting charge was just enough to break open the casing and allow the phosphorus to escape. It then ignited spontaneously on contact with the atmosphere, producing a characteristic thick white smoke cloud.

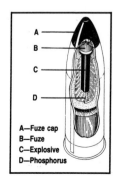

A—Fuze cap
B—Fuze
C—Explosive
D—Phosphorus

Call in the artillery

SMART OUTFIT: An immaculate M-102 of B Battery, 3/19th Artillery, ready and prepared for action—and a general's inspection. The men have even picked out in white paint the serial numbers on the M-109's Firestone tires. Clearly visible is the "speed shift" pivot between the wheels and the springs for the recoil-absorbing mechanism.

to repoint the weapon, the crew had to lower the howitzer off its firing jack, the heavy trails had to be lifted, and the howitzer had to be pointed by hand. This operation required at least eight men. When the ground was muddy, a typical environment in the monsoon climate, it was especially difficult.

Early in the war Lieutenant Nathaniel Foster of the 8th Battalion, 6th Artillery, 1st Infantry Division, tackled this problem and devised a solution. He locally manufactured a metal pedestal and placed it under the howitzer's carriage at the balance point. The howitzer's weight was then supported almost as if it were sitting on a jack. When

the piece had to be repointed, the howitzer was lowered to rest on the pedestal. Then the crew could pick up the trails and swing the howitzer about to face the new direction. This speed shift could be performed by as few as four men. It took only seconds. Because the howitzer's weight rested on the pedestal, the crew could shift the piece without great physical labor. During one demanding 19-hour period, a howitzer in Foster's battery was speed shifted 33 times without reducing the crew's effectiveness due to exhaustion.

As a result of the terrain and the enemy's tactics in Vietnam, a typical small-unit engagement began

Front line —A Marine forward artillery observer (FO) scans the jungle for potential enemy targets. Patrolling with the infantry, he was the artillery's link with the front line. In an ambush the enemy would try to take out the radio telephone operator (RTO) first, before he could summon artillery and air strikes.

at extremely close range—under 50 meters, often as close as 10. It lasted for only ten minutes. Then the enemy broke contact and ran to evade the American firestorm of artillery and aerial bombardment. Under these conditions American platoon and company leaders struggled to figure out how best to use their artillery support.

An American infantry battalion might be out on an operation for 15 to 20 days. They returned to a fire support base for a three-day break. At this time junior leaders, particularly the second lieutenants who served as forward artillery observers (FOs) compared experiences and talked to the gunners about how best to coordinate future efforts. Over time infantry who operated with the same artillery learned about a battery's ability: how quickly could they respond, how accurate was their fire, how confident were they at delivering very close support? There was no substitute for such experience.

During training infantry officers were given basic instruction about artillery and how to call for it. The training included at least one practical session; hunkered down in a bunker, the green lieutenants would call in artillery fire, hear it whistle directly over their heads, and watch it explode nearby.

Entering the field in Vietnam each infantry company had a forward observer assigned to it, who was in radio contact with the nearest artillery battery. The FO, as an artilleryman, would be the units' acknowledged technical expert for calling in the guns. Normally he would stay close to the company commander so together they could provide central direction. Serving with the FO would be a recon sergeant, a specialist trained in the use of artillery. Whenever a company was split into three or four maneuver elements, the platoon leaders of the units without a specialist had to handle their own fire support missions.

Such responsibility became easier with time but during a junior officer's first missions it was all he could do to follow instructions and move from point A to point B. The terrain, with easily identifiable landmarks often obscured by the seemingly endless jungle, could easily disorient a newcomer. Operating out of sight from friendly units, a platoon could quickly find itself lost if the leader was inexperienced. There were no reference points in the

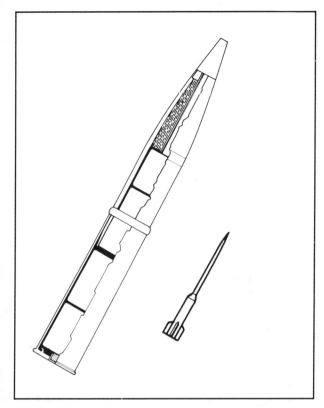

The M-546 "beehive" round had a two-piece body of aluminum, loaded with 8,000 steel flechette darts. When the clockwork time fuze detonated, four charges at the front of the shell ripped open the casing, and the spin of the shell began to scatter the flechettes. At the same time, flame from the charges flashed down the central tube, igniting the base charge and forcing the remaining darts foward and out through the torn casing. The first beehive used in combat killed nine enemy infantry and stopped an attack. It gained its name from the deadly sound made by the hail of darts as they spun through the air.

jungle. Platoon leaders relate that they spent entire first missions being lost. In spite of advanced communications, the practice of sending a man up a tree to search for a familiar landmark was not uncommon.

At times like this the artillery provided a new service.

The platoon leader requested a "marking mission." Standard training dictated that such a mission should aim at an easily identifiable terrain feature. In triple canopy jungle there was no such target. Instead the artillery fired at a grid coordinate, an intersection of two lines on the map. The gunners loaded white phosphorous ("Willie Peter") shells set to burst 100 meters up in the air. Willie Peter shells burst with a brilliant white explosion easily seen from a distance. So a unit uncertain of its location, or completely lost, radioed the request to a battery: ". . .Willie Peter, 100 hanging."

"Splash over," the battery would respond—the

Call in the artillery

QUICK REACTION:
A top-line 105mm battery could have 36 rounds in the air before the first one hit the ground and the enemy had begun to run for cover. Here, A Battery, 3/13 Artillery, is firing flat out in support of the 4th Battalion, 9th Infantry, near Cu Chi in October 1968. The flow of the crew's work is clockwise. The two men at right are screwing fuzes into shells, which are passed around the chain to the loader (facing camera, left center). The request for supporting fire had come so fast that the men had not yet had time to dig in.

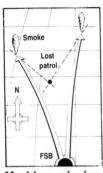

Marking mission —Artillery proved invaluable in the jungle in helping lost units locate their positions. A lost patrol would radio for artillery to fire smoke shells overhead at a map coordinate —a point where two grid lines intersect. The platoon leader would watch for the shell smoke, point his compass toward it, estimate its distance, and then draw a line on his map along the compass reading through the map coordinate. A second marking mission would give the position accurately.

shell was on its way. Then came the explosion. A flower-like plume of white smoke would spread out against the blue sky. The platoon leader would point his compass toward the plume and estimate the distance. Then he drew a line on his map along the compass bearing. Next he requested a second marking mission directed at another grid intersection. The gunners would comply with a white phosphorous air burst. Again using his compass the leader would draw a second line on his map. His position was where the two lines intersected. The company could then resume its plodding progress through the jungle.

The marking missions oriented a lost unit with surprising accuracy. One FO at base used this technique to plot a position near the perimeter. A survey party checked his calculations. He had placed the position to within 10 meters of the true location. During daytime operations frequent marking missions proved indispensable in order to keep units from getting lost.

Once a unit knew where it was, it had to work to keep from getting lost again. Either the platoon leader or the FO marched on a compass bearing while another soldier, the "pacer," counted the number of steps traveled. Some placed a pebble in their pockets every hundred paces in order to keep track of distance. Although tremendous technical military advances had occurred, the drummers who tapped out the cadence controlling the march of Frederick the Great's Prussian grenadiers and their file closers who regulated the length of the men's stride would have well understood the procedures used by American soldiers in the jungles of Vietnam.

As a patrol advanced an experienced officer made mental adjustments in case he had to suddenly summon artillery help. Some units required a radio check of position every ten minutes. In addition to such safeguards, a combat veteran anticipated where contacts might occur. He had the appropriate map coordinates precalculated in order to speed up the process of calling for artillery. Some officers abdicated this responsibility to the FOs and recon sergeants. They figured they had enough to attend to just keeping the men vigilant and ready for combat.

Regardless, once combat began, knowing exactly

where you were might make the difference between life and death. Such knowledge permitted the platoon leader or the FO to immediately call for help. The enemy realized this as well. They concentrated their fire on the leaders and the radiomen (radio-telephone operators, or RTOs). The former were obvious because they were the ones shouting out instructions. The latter could be easily pinpointed by the long radio aerials extending up into the air. These command groups were favorite sniper targets.

Usually a platoon had two radios. If the RTOs and

ON STANDBY:
A weary battery Air Cav 105 crew clears up shell cases from the night before and stacks ammunition ready for their next fire mission.

First team —Insignia of the the 1st Cavalry Division (Airmobile). Aggressive in its use of artillery, the 1st Cav was equipped with M-102 105mm towed howitzers and rocket-armed Huey helicopters. The howitzers were lifted into combat by the division's own CH-47 Chinook medium-lift helicopters. A complete six-gun 105mm battery with its ammunition could be moved in just 11 Chinook sorties.

platoon leaders lived through the first fire, and if a radio message could be transmitted—a chancy proposition when maneuvering in triple canopy jungle or in mountainous terrain—then the infantry could call for artillery support.

The first shells normally fell at least 600 meters from the American front line. This distance left a safety margin in case either the unit had misplotted its position or the artillerymen made an aiming error. Sometimes the fire stayed at this distance in hopes of interdicting enemy reinforcements. Calling for closer support required special procedures. This was "danger close," a term that indicated the shells were to break near friendly troops. In some units the field leader had to provide his initials along with the firing request. This meant that the leader specifically authorized close-in artillery bombardment.

The leader would observe the fall of shot and radio corrections. When firing requests asked for the shells to break inside 200 meters of the front line, the artillerymen tended to get understandably jumpy. A fractional error—a slightly defective shell or a sudden wind gust—could bring the fire directly in on your own men.

The way artillery was used depended on the aggressiveness of the combat unit. A gung-ho outfit like the Air Cav, led by an aggressive officer, might call for an artillery barrage behind the enemy's position and then attack in an effort to force the enemy into the barrage. A more cautious commander might request the artillery several hundred meters to his front, fall back, adjust the artillery in closer, and try to eliminate the enemy with artillery fire alone. This sort of tactic became more prevalent as the war progressed and orders came from the high command to keep American losses low.

Combat leaders partially based their calls for artillery on their assessment of the battery's competence. In addition, the type of artillery available influenced the decision. Larger guns firing bigger shells needed a greater margin for error since the lethal zone of an 8-inch howitzer, about 75 meters in open terrain, exceeded the 30-meter zone of the 105mm shell.

In an ambush, the most common beginning to a combat, an experienced officer would immediately

Call in the artillery

TARGET ACQUISITION:
A member of Battery F, 26th Artillery, uses a powerful binocular periscope to spot the enemy in the Demilitarized Zone. One of the main difficulties facing artillery in Vietnam was target acquisition —finding the enemy. NVA gunners firing across the zone knew that US firepower would wipe them out if they betrayed their presence, and used camouflage skills and irregular firing times to remain concealed.

Call in the artillery

HIGH VISIBILITY: This mountain view shows exactly why so many FSBs were located on hilltops. The two black marker posts with "1600" and "2400" in white on them are part of the millivadier system used by artillerymen to exactly locate their firing position. A complete circle was 6,400 mils—the Vietnam artilleryman's firing environment.

try to direct his men to hit the enemy's flanks. Simultaneously he assessed the enemy's volume of fire; the VC typically fired quickly and ran. The appropriate artillery response was to call for the shells to break behind the enemy's position to catch him as he fled.

The better disciplined NVA regulars used aimed fire and thus shot slower. When under such fire, the combat leader knew he was in for a longer fight. Consequently he would call for the artillery to break directly over the enemy position.

When a ground unit finished its daytime maneuvers it settled in for nighttime defense. The

unit called for artillery registration shots along all four compass points. The initial rounds hit at 1,000 meters out. The fires were adjusted in to 600 meters. Thus, should the enemy launch an attack, both the foot sloggers and the artillerymen knew the coordinates so they could fire immediately.

With this high level of support the ground combat troops in Vietnam valued their artillery backup. One platoon leader remembered the artillerymen as "very professional, precise, and motivated." But he couldn't resist noting that "they were a bit hung up on creature comforts at their fire support bases."

Anatomy of a mission

5

How a gun battery operated

A FIRE MISSION started with a call on the radio. Picking up the receiver, the battery exec or the chief of battery heard the words that never failed to excite an artilleryman: "Fire mission, battery adjust, two, four, hundred." The exec repeated the order to ensure he heard it correctly and then telephoned it to each gun in the six-gun 155mm battery. His call prompted the crew to start a sequence of carefully rehearsed moves.

Most batteries in Vietnam had to make do with five men per gun, though seven-man crews were standard operating procedure. The batteries in Vietnam usually managed with a chief of section, gunner, assistant gunner, loader, and powder man. While two men could operate the gun, five seasoned artillerymen could maintain peak performance over an extended period. The big guns rested on a special pedestal with a welded ball-and-joint mechanism. Two men lifting each trail hefted the gun until the trails rested in premeasured slots corresponding to the ordered direction. Because of the finely balanced pedestal each man had to lift a load of only about 50 pounds.

The crew jacked the piece off the pedestal onto the firing jack while the chief of section confirmed the firing data. Meanwhile the battery exec ran to the aiming circle. The aiming circle was a device like an engineer's transit equipped with a scope capable of both day and night viewing. The exec used the aiming circle to "survey in" each gun. During this surveying procedure, each gunner pointed a telescope at the aiming circle. Using the aiming circle as a reference point the gunner made sure his gun tube was pointed in the right direction. When all six gunners finished, the battery was properly laid for

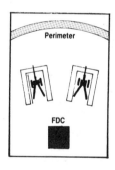

direction. By this time the fire direction center (FDC) should have correctly calculated the deflection (the exact bearing) and elevation. The FDC personnel used two charts laid out on tables. These firing and check charts gave the center the appearance of a draftsman's work area. Hovering over the charts, equipped with a long protractor-like rule, the chart operators determined deflection, range, and altitude. Other soldiers, known as "computers," converted this initial data to firing data for the guns. One soldier carried out the calculation to be used by the guns while the other performed the same calculation as a check.

Around mid-1968 electronic computers began to replace the human computers who acted as checkers. If the twin calculations were within two or three mils (a one-mil difference at 10,000 meters made a difference of about 10 meters on the ground) the data were relayed to the battery exec. When the computers determined the range a simple cross reference indicated the optimal powder charge needed to propel the shell the required distance. If the calculations weren't within two or three mils the computers repeated the math. Because numerous important mathematical calculations were performed at the

HOWITZER PIT:
A semi-permanent 105mm self-propelled howitzer emplacement of the type found on most FSBs. Inside the sandbag wall, ammunition was racked neatly into sections for HE, ICM, illumination, chemical, and propaganda shells. The extension on the right provided quarters for the gun crew.

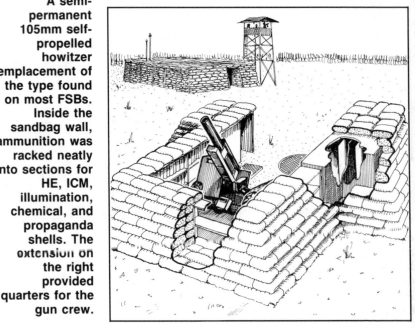

FDC, often under time pressure, the center's personnel were handpicked from the brightest soldiers.

Calculations complete, the FDC provided the firing data to each gun. Around each weapon one could tell the old timers from the new guys. If you shouted to a veteran while he was working the gun he wouldn't respond. He couldn't hear, the constant din of combat had partially ruined his hearing. Although the crew had earplugs they seldom wore them. When a divisional artillery general introduced

The right angle —In the fire detection center at FSB Tomahawk a chart operator works out the range of the target while computers, both human and electronic, work out firing data for transmission to the guns.

navy-type earmuffs, he noticed the only time they were worn was inside the bunkers when the crew tried to sleep.

Seated to the left of the gun tube the gunner turned a large crank to precisely set the deflection, using aiming stakes set in front of each gun. Next the assistant gunner adjusted the tube's elevation. When the deflection and elevation were properly set, both the telescope and the bubbles inside the levels attached to the gun were correctly aligned.

The chief of the firing section also received information about the shell type and fuze. While the assistant gunner "leveled the bubbles" the assistant gunner inserted a primer into the firing lock. The fist-sized firing lock screwed into the breech. The loader went to the ammunition bunker to get the correct shell. Then he tightened the fuze into the shell's nose and prepared to assist in loading.

The choice of fuze was important. A "quick" fuze exploded as soon as it hit anything, either dense vegetation covering the land or the ground itself. A "variable time" fuze used a radar signal to determine when the shell was 20 meters above the ground. Then it would explode. Artillerymen considered this the most reliable fuze for air bursts since it detonated, if set reasonably accurately, only when it was 20 meters directly over the target (although a heavy rain could produce a false reading, causing the shell to explode prematurely).

The mission could also call for a time fuze. In this event the loader exactly set the number of seconds until the shell exploded. This was a dicey proposition. Although the FDC personnel tried to compensate for all factors, such things as the wind, density of the air, temperature, humidity, and weather influenced a shell's time of flight.

Decisions regarding the type of fuze were important and were made by the FO in the field and the fire direction center. Fuze in place, the loader carried the 95-pound round to the gun's breech. Aided by the assistant gunner, the loader used a rammer staff, a long plunger, to push the shell up into the tube's rifling where it stuck. The rifled grooves inside the barrel held the shell tightly creating a seal.

While this was happening the powder man went to the powder canister (a long, sealed container designed to keep the powder dry) and hauled out a

DIGITAL DIRECTION: In a fire detection center a computer operator works with his Field Artillery Digital Automatic Computer (FADAC) to calculate the range of the target before transmission to the guns. One of the many advantages of the FADAC data processor, introduced in 1968, was its ability to record all the firing data for future reference.

full powder charge. Each bag housed seven incremental charges. All seven sent the shell to its maximum range removing a charge decreased the range.

The powder man carried the appropriate number of charges to the gun and inserted the bag into the breech. On the bottom of each bag lay an easily ignitable firing pad. The primer ignited this pad, thus burning the powder and sending the shell on its way. At the command "Close!" the assistant gunner positioned to the right of the barrel closed the breech, secured the firing lock, and held the lanyard. Everyone else moved away.

The section chief supervised the entire operation to ensure everyone performed his task correctly. He watched the loader to make sure he had brought the right shell with the correct fuze. If a time fuze was needed the loader showed it to the chief of section to

An FDC's radio operator (above) calls quadrants and range to the battery chief at his aiming circle (below) who then works with each gun in the battery in turn to calculate the correct azimuth bearing to lay the gun on. Magnetic compasses couldn't be used because the guns were made of steel. The loudspeaker fitted to the FDC's radio ensured that all the FDC personnel heard the instructions and mistakes could be detected.

verify the time setting before loading the shell. Similarly, the powder man held unused charges until the gun fired to confirm that the proper number of charges were used. The chief also looked through the telescope to make sure it was lined up on the aiming stakes. Finally he set a hand-held level parallel to the breech as a separate check on the gun's elevation. Before the gun fired, the section chief would have supervised every mechanical and arithmetic step.

The battery exec shouted out a last sequence of commands: "Battery!" and each section chief shouted back his gun's number. Thus the exec knew all six guns were ready to fire. Often the battery fired simultaneously since the blast of six shells exploding simultaneously was greater than separate explosions. Having verified each gun's readiness he gave the last order: "Fire!" Six men pulled six lanyards and the shells went on their way.

Even when the entire battery had a fire mission, initial adjustments involved only two guns. The forward observer radioed back corrections until the shells landed within 50 meters of the target. With a final adjustment the full battery fired.

Throughout the entire operation all possible safety procedures were employed. Everything was read back from the listener to the speaker to verify the message was understood. All numerical data were said by individual digit ("one, three, five" rather than "one hundred thirty five") and all alphabetical data were said phonetically ("delta tango" rather than "DT").

In order to ensure that all friendly forces operated under the artillery umbrella, the artillery was usually dispersed to a greater extent than in previous wars. A battery might never be positioned with its sister batteries in the battalion. A single battery might even be split into sections and stationed in separate locations. Such dispersal placed more responsibility on the junior officers. Isolated from the rest of the battery, they could not rely upon more experienced senior officers for guidance. As one senior veteran officer noted: "This war, at least from the field artillery point of view, is largely a battery commander's war—the junior officer must really be on his toes, thinking ahead, and he must be self-reliant."

Anatomy of a mission

READY TO LOAD:

105mm rounds are assembled (top) and fuzes are screwed into the nose of the shell, which is in turn placed into the brass case holding the propellant charge. A high explosive shell (center), weighing 95 pounds, is carried to a 155mm howitzer. Lastly, the powder charge is placed in the breech of an 8-inch gun (below).

83

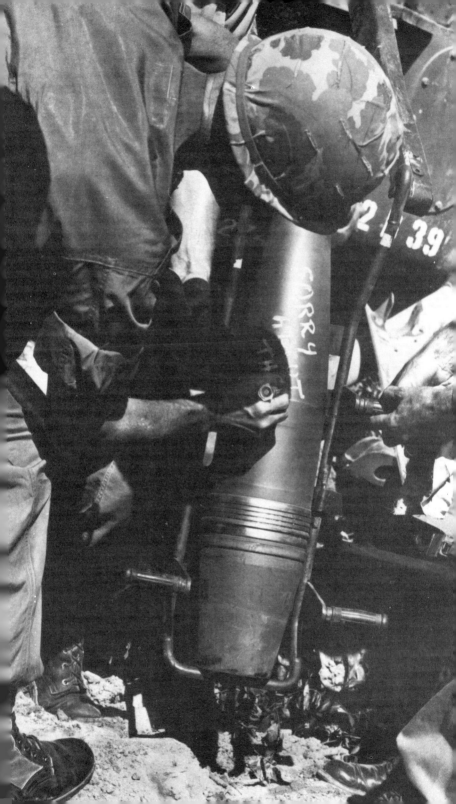

Friendly fire

Shooting the doughnut

GIVEN THE DIFFICULTY of target acquisition, and the need for duplicate safety checks, many artillery batteries averaged about a five-minute response time to requests for fire. Some batteries responded in under two minutes. The Marines at Khe Sanh managed to reduce this to an incredible 40 seconds. However, in spite of the safety checks, whenever artillery fired something could go wrong.

In one such accident an FO had established where the supporting battery was to fire in case his company was attacked during the night. When the attack came, the FO requested a 100-meter shift away from the previously designated target. The battery believed that the company was under a critical threat and thus fired a contact mission rather than gradually adjusting its fire. Its shells landed inside the company perimeter, killing 3 and wounding 19 Americans.

In the investigation that followed, several critical errors were discovered. The original target turned out to be much closer to the company than the FO had supposed. He had misjudged because of the dense jungle and the darkness. The FO had thought the enemy attack was more dangerous than it really was and had dispensed with the normal firing adjustments that would have revealed his first mistake. The battery had fired accurately but the FO's compound error had caused the shells to hit friendly troops.

In another incident an FO, under sniper fire, called for an artillery marking mission. He planned to "walk" the rounds in on the enemy position. The first shell landed some 600 meters away, roughly where the FO wanted it. He radioed: "Drop 400, repeat, one round." The second round landed right

Friendly fire

FIRE:
This double exposure shows a II Corps gunner running to his 175mm M-107 gun, then pulling the lanyard to send the shell on its way. The 175mm was least accurate at short ranges. Its theoretical maximum range was reached when it was at 45 degrees elevation.

next to the FO, killing both him and his radioman. The investigation determined that the firing battery had not shot for some time and consequently the gun tubes were cold. The artillery manuals stated that the first round from a cold tube would be long—thus the first shell seemed to be safely off in the distance. The manual went on to explain that the second round from a cold tube would be short. Someone had forgotten and two soldiers had died.

Analysis of all such incidents for 1967 revealed that artillery caused by far the greatest number of friendly casualties: more than aircraft, small arms, or any other source. The most common cause was fire direction center and firing battery errors, followed

by faulty ammunition, poorly coordinated communication, unit disorientation, and observer error.

In past wars the artillery usually shot over the lines into enemy territory. If the shells didn't land precisely where aimed they still struck enemy territory. In Vietnam the guns frequently had to "shoot into the doughnut," a small target circle surrounded by friendly troops. Neither "overs" nor "shorts" could be tolerated. Coupled with the difficult terrain and the enemy's "hugging" tactics the likelihood of error increased.

Another novel aspect of the Vietnam War was the extent to which the airspace over the battlefield was crowded. Ground attack aircraft, helicopters, and

CHECK FIRE: The gunner's warning hand stops a round going into the breech. The cease-fire order could mean friendly troops had advanced into the target zone. The massive spades on the end of the towing trails have dug deep furrows in the soft ground while this 105mm was firing. The howitzer will be resurveyed for each fire mission.

artillery shells all claimed a portion of the sky. The artillery hated suspending fire in order to permit the aircraft to dive-bomb a target. If they ceased fire they would give the enemy target a valuable reprieve. However, elaborate coordination was needed.

Various "Save a Plane" checks and clearances were employed. But they were not always successfully implemented. On one occasion a 155mm battery was pounding a target when the bombers arrived. The air controller correctly directed the bombers to turn at a certain spot in order to avoid the artillery that was firing against one end of the target. All except the last plane made the proper turn. This plane flew straight for too long and a shell blew its tail off. As the plane spiraled to the ground, first one crew member and then another ejected. The first crewman's parachute opened and he was safely recovered by ground troops. The second man's chute only opened as he hit the ground.

In addition to the always lurking possibility of hitting friendly troops, artillerymen themselves worked in a risky environment. They operated heavy equipment and handled explosives. Fatigue, carelessness, stupidity, or just bad luck sometimes had lethal results.

Fatigue was presumed to be the cause when a 1st Division 155mm howitzer exploded, killing its crew. Investigators, including the divisional artillery commander, examined the wreckage. A swab used for cleaning the tube still stood in a bucket near the gun. Closer inspection showed that the bucket was empty with only a thick mud slime remaining in the bottom. Since there was no water in the bucket, the crew couldn't have been cleaning the tube after each shot. Apparently the crew had rammed the round home and tossed in a powder charge. A bit of hot debris from the previous blast had ignited the charge. They knew they shouldn't have done this but they were tired. Trying to take a shortcut, they died.

Carelessness seemed to be the culprit in a series of catastrophic explosions that knocked out several self-propelled howitzers. In order to get a good shell spread, the guns—whether self-propelled or towed—were distributed on the ground in a staggered formation. Consequently some guns to the rear fired over the heads of those in front. In a self-propelled battery a crewman would have the next round ready outside the vehicle while he waited for the gun to fire. He would toss unused powder charges onto the ground nearby.

Sometimes a small trace of burning powder would shoot out the barrel after a gun fired. When this happened from a howitzer positioned behind another howitzer, the embers might fall on either the ready charge held by the crewman or on the discarded charges at his feet. The resulting explosion reduced the large self-propelled gun into a heap of molten metal three feet high. Eventually procedures were changed and such incidents ended. The guns were redistributed on the ground. For a six-gun battery, a five pointed star-shaped formation to provide an effective pattern of ground bursts with the sixth piece in the middle to fire illumination rounds was a favorite configuration.

But even being in the center of a battery could be dangerous. One night the commander of a battery of towed 105mm howitzers was awakened from a deep sleep in the early hours of the morning. His exec told him an urgent fire mission was

Cleaning out —Marines at Con Thien ram a swab into the barrel of a 105mm howitzer. Proper maintenance and upkeep were vital. Most accidents occurred when the pressure of combat was too great and units failed to observe proper procedures.

Friendly fire

BIRD-DOG: Pilot and artillery observer (AO) of the 184th Aviation Company in an 01 Bird-Dog looking for targets while standing by for a contact mission. The slow, high-wing 01 could stay in contact with a potential target by stretching out its fuel for up to five hours. For marking targets it carried two 3.5-inch white phosphorus rockets on each wing.

needed. Wiping sleep from his eyes the commander staggered up the ladder leading to a tower from which the battery could be properly aimed. The tower had telephone communication with the fire direction center and was in the middle of the battery position. The commander received and transmitted orders and proudly watched his men respond with practiced skill. They moved the trails to aim the weapons and elevate the tubes. Concentrating on the task at hand, caught up in the excitement, and still somewhat groggy, the commander only realized at the last second that one of the pieces

was pointing directly over his tower! The last word he heard through the telephone was "Fire!"

The concussive muzzle blast slammed him against the far wall. Picking himself up, the commander sheepishly descended the ladder. Fortunately, only a severe headache and a persistent ringing of the ears punished him for his carelessness.

Simple stupidity was the cause of some accidents. As one divisional artillery commander explained it, "none of us figured it out at first, although we should have."

The problem seemed to happen at night when it

After the stall
—The job of an
AO was not
without hazard.
This O1
Bird-Dog
experienced
engine failure
due to a
contaminated
fuel line. The
pilot stalled the
aircraft after
losing power
over the trees,
before it fell
nose first into
the treetops.
The pilot, flying
alone, suffered
only cuts on his
knees as the
instrument
panel was
pushed back.
The crew
compartment
stayed intact—a
relief to his AO,
who flew back
seat.

was raining and only one man was working each gun. The crewman would be given a deflection and elevation over the telephone, say "1,500 mils." The gun had two scales running from 0 to 3,200 mils. He had to figure out which scale his firing data referred to. In poor visibility it was easy to make a mistake. This setup was the cause of many shells landing 180 degrees in the wrong direction.

Only after enough friendly troops were hit, did investigators figure out the problem. It turned out the calibration system came from the Army, copying the French 75mm system made famous in World War I. Subsequent American artillery designers kept the system, which worked well enough in past wars with defined front lines. Only when the artillery had to fire in a 360-degree (or 6,400-mil) environment did the problem arise.

Individuals could do bone-headed things, some of which were deadly while others were merely comical. One time at a 1st Division fire support base three artillery battalions had fired all night long. As usual, the morning's cleanup involved a bulldozer digging a trench for burning trash. Some artillerymen loaded unexpended powder charges into a truck for disposal. Feeling lazy, they backed the truck up against the trench. Nearby, the divisional artillery commander, General Lawrence C. Caruthers, was inspecting the base, along with his boss, the division commander. The divisional commander was well known for his temper and his willingness to relieve subordinates on the spot when he thought they had messed up. As the two generals talked the artillerymen shoveled the first load of powder into the trench. The shovelful caught fire and flamed.

Immediately the soldiers dived away from the truck as the fire spread to the back of the open truck and reached the entire powder load. The briskly burning truck attracted the generals' attention.

"Now just what in the hell is going on, Caruthers?" snapped the division commander. Conducting a mini-investigation around the blackened vehicle, General Caruthers managed to sort things out. With some difficulty he explained to his superior what had happened. Since no one had been injured the incident passed; funny with hindsight, embarrassing at the time.

Finally, simple bad luck caused occasional friendly

casualties. An artillery commander, hearing that a soldier had been hit by friendly fire, landed his helicopter and investigated. A lightly wounded private apologetically explained what had happened: "Sir, I'm sorry, I'm sorry. I heard that thing coming and I could have ducked in time. I just didn't." When close support artillery fire landed, friendly troops had to react quickly and hit the dirt. This soldier had frozen for a brief moment and a metal fragment had torn off a chunk of muscle and flesh in his forearm.

Fatigue, carelessness, stupidity, and bad luck killed and maimed both friendly troops and innocent civilians. The artillerymen worked hard to prevent it. Yet the accuracy required for the artillery in this war was something new.

The village of Ben Cat, for example, had been hit several times by errant American artillery. It caused political uproar and the artillery battalion commander caught the devil whenever this happened. He eventually solved the problem by setting up stakes in front of each gun. He told the crew not to fire when the tube was pointed between these stakes. In this way the guns could never be pointed at the village. The system became known as the "Ben Cat stakes" and proved to be a field expedient that worked.

THE BUBBLE: The OH-13, known as the "Bubble," was the first helicopter to be used by divisional artillery observers when they arrived in Vietnam in 1965. Later it was replaced by the purpose-built OH-6A, known as the Loach after the abbreviation LOH (Light Observation Helicopter). The OH-6A was faster, had armor-plated seats, and could carry four people.

93

Bullets, not bodies

"Use bullets, not bodies."

**Firepower
saves lives**

THE WORDS ran through the captain's head as he and his men lay on their stomachs searching the silent wall of green that surrounded them. The patrol of the 173d Airborne had run into an enemy force of unknown size. The action began when a single shot whizzed past the point man leading the company. Now all was quiet.

The captain considered what might be in front of them: a sniper or a sizeable enemy force? He had no way of knowing. Then he recalled General Williamson's words about sparing the men by using bullets. Earlier in the unit's tour eager American soldiers had aggressively charged enemy positions when facing the unknown. Several units suffered heavy losses from the resulting ambush. The captain decided to be more cautious. He would conduct what was known as a "reconnaissance by fire."

While the paratroopers deployed in line to fire their rifles, the forward artillery observer called the supporting artillery battery. The FO provided firing data so the guns could fire a marking round 600 meters in front of the American patrol.

Meanwhile, the captain ordered his men to open fire. As their 30 rifles and two machine guns blindly fired into the jungle, several shattering explosions shook the earth. Momentarily stunned, the captain ordered his FO to request artillery support. Anticipating this order, the FO had already called for the fire mission. He adjusted the fire and began bringing the shells closer to the American front line. The battalion commander watched the action from his command helicopter. He ordered the captain to

**Insignia of the
173d Airborne**

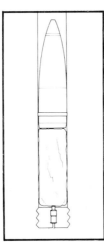

Firing procedure —A cutaway showing the inside of a 155mm howitzer barrel. The shell was loaded first and then a separate charge, a bag of propellant, was stuffed in behind it. The breech was screwed in and an electrically primed cartridge inserted. When the primer went off, the propellant ignited and the shell shot out the barrel.

pull his men back so the artillery could shell positions even nearer the American line. As the paratroopers withdrew, the artillery barrage deluged the supposed enemy position. The battalion commander saw red smoke mixed with the shell bursts. Were his own men trying to signal with smoke grenades that they were being hit? Since the enemy often used smoke to deceive American artillery observers, the commander called his captain: "Are your men popping red smoke?"

"No," came the reply and the relieved commander called in an air strike to supplement the artillery. Clearly the enemy was releasing the smoke in an effort to make the Americans call off the attack.

Later, as the officers discussed the operation, they concluded that the initial enemy shot had been an attempt to lure the paratroopers forward. The enemy would allow the Americans to enter the killing zone where his mines would decimate them. Instead, the paratroopers' random rifle fire panicked the foe into prematurely detonating the mines. These had been the tremendous explosions that had started the fight. No Americans had been hit in the engagement. Whether the artillery and air strikes hit anything no one knew. But everyone agreed the "recon by fire" had been the tactic that had kept the patrol clear of an enemy trap.

Again American firepower—a platoon volley, an artillery bombardment, and an air strike in response to a single rifle shot—had saved American lives.

As the doctrine of "bullets, not bodies" took root, combat units became increasingly more sophisticated in the use of massed firepower. But every step forward was met by enemy counter-measures and avoidance tactics. One classic action, later to become a textbook example of escalating firepower, involved various companies of the 1st Battalion, 2d Brigade, 25th Infantry Division. For four days they had tried to assault a large abandoned village. Air strikes followed by an artillery bombardment followed by a ground assault had been the pattern and it hadn't worked. One company suffered 15 casualties in three futile hours. Captain Jimmie Adams decided to try something different.

Rows of bamboo thickets divided the L-shaped village into separate sections centered on individual houses. Around the village lay cultivated rice

Bullets, not bodies

BULLETS, NOT BODIES:

A forest of 155mm shells are stood on end, then fuzed and stacked ready for Operation Junction City, one of the big sweeps of 1967. Without sufficient infantry to occupy a hostile countryside, the US high command relied on setting up a network of firebases, within whose range friendly forces could expect to win firefights by sheer weight of explosive. The catch was that more and more resources had to go into supplying and defending the firebases.

97

175mm shells fuzed and ready for a shoot into the DMZ in August 1967. The 20-mile range of the M-107 gave it a good reach into enemy territory, when a target could be found.

paddies to the west and north while a rubber plantation bordered the north and east. The Americans suspected that a tunnel complex ran along the village's northern border.

Captain Adams felt that a successful assault would have to rely on well-organized firepower. Toward that end he sat down with his weapons platoon leader and his forward observer, Lieutenant Ed Brickman, to develop a detailed fire plan. Adams thought that during previous attacks the enemy had sheltered in the tunnel complex and then surfaced to fire at the Americans once the bombardment stopped.

Accordingly he had Brickman arrange for 105mm howitzer fire to start in the southernmost portion of the village and walk slowly to the north. The infantry would follow hard on the heels of the breaking shells. The company's 81mm mortars would shell the tunnel complex area shortly after the howitzers opened fire. Adams hoped this slight delay would catch the enemy running for the sheltering tunnels. Heavier mortars belonging to the battalion would shell a patch of bamboo that had hidden enemy snipers during previous assaults.

Once the infantry gained the village all weapons except the heavy mortars would begin harassing and interdiction fire to the north while the big 4.2-inch mortars waited in reserve. Finally Adams arranged for helicopter gunships to be available should they be needed.

With everything ready the first howitzer shells shrieked overhead toward the village. The men moved forward. An explosion rocked the lead platoon and someone cried "Short round!" The unit began to panic. A quick-thinking sergeant recognized that this was an enemy mortar round and not a mis-aimed American artillery shell. He remembered that their recent training in Hawaii had warned that the enemy sometimes tried to simulate a short round in an effort to get the Americans to stop their own fire. The sergeant calmed his men. As they advanced they heard enemy soldiers shouting as they tried to flee from the artillery bombardment. But the mortar fire raking the tunnel complex prevented them from finding shelter. The infantry gained the village. As the enemy withdrew, the Americans searched the houses for enemy supplies. They found

very little: only one enemy body and a few sacks of rice. Burning the village as they withdrew they took comfort in the fact that they succeeded where others had failed. Furthermore, because of the well-conceived, well-executed fire plan no American soldier had been hit during the attack.

However, the "bullets, not bodies" doctrine became meaningless when the enemy managed to hug in too close to US lines. One such occasion occurred close to dawn on 15 October 1967, when the NVA attacked Battery A, 2d Battalion, 320th Artillery, 101st Airborne Division, with a deadly mixture of mortar, recoilless rifle, rocket-propelled grenade, and machine gun fire. As the defenders ran to their guns, the North Vietnamese broke through the battery's defensive perimeter. They began systematically hand grenading the artillery pits. Sergeant Webster Anderson, chief of section in Battery A, mounted the exposed parapet of his gun position and began aggressively directing its defense. Disregarding his own safety, the sergeant directed his howitzer's fire at point-blank range against the attackers. While calling out targets for his gun, he saw NVA soldiers, who had evaded the

BATTLEGROUND:
Men of the 2/9 Artillery firing at NVA regulars in a battle with the 25th Infantry Division during Operation Paul Revere. Gunners rarely had the chance to shoot at such a major target.

Bullets, not bodies

CLOSE SUPPORT: A 2/1 Marines 60mm mortar crew fires into a suspected ambush site. The 60mm looks puny compared to the big guns of the field artillery, but it was always ready for use, and at 30 rounds a minute it could deliver a significant punch in an ambush. Its main disadvantage was lack of range—maximum was just over a mile.

artillery fire, nearing the firing pit. Perched atop the sandbags, Anderson hurled grenades and fired his rifle. His one-man defense saved the gun. Two enemy grenades landed at his feet, exploded, and knocked him down with severe leg wounds. Unable to stand and in great pain, Anderson propped himself against the parapet and continued to direct howitzer fire against the enemy. His fighting spirit greatly encouraged the gun crew.

What followed is best described on the honor citation for Sergeant Anderson: "Seeing an enemy grenade land within the gun pit near a wounded

member of his gun crew, Sergeant Anderson, heedless of his own safety, seized the grenade and attempted to throw it over the parapet to save his men. . . it exploded and Sergeant Anderson was again grievously wounded. Although only partially conscious and severely wounded, Sergeant Anderson refused medical evacuation and continued to encourage his men in the defense of the position."

For his extraordinary heroism "at the risk of his own life above and beyond the call of duty," Sergeant Webster Anderson received the Medal of Honor.

The view from above

The fire support base policy

THE 20-YEAR GAP between the end of World War II and the buildup of American forces in Vietnam saw the career artillery officers who served in combat against the Germans and Japanese climb the promotion ladder. Gunners of World War II were the policy-makers in Vietnam. Others served in important command positions. In their place, a new generation of soldiers manned the guns.

One combat veteran of World War II was Brigadier General Willis Crittenberger who led the II Field Force Artillery. This command served as the corps artillery for forces fighting in the III Corps Zone, an area extending from around Saigon out to the Cambodian border. The heavy guns of the corps artillery acted as a strategic reserve, available to support operations throughout the III Corps. Crittenberger's job was to ensure that the reserve went where it was needed to assist the American 1st and 25th Divisions as well as ARVN units, and that it contributed to the fighting once it got there.

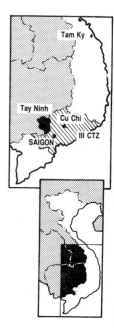

Like most American officers, the general's training had stressed preparation for fighting a conventional war against the Russians in Europe. But he felt this training was relevant to the area war being fought in Vietnam. In Europe, NATO forces recognized they could not fight on an inflexible front if attacked by the much larger Communist forces. Rather, it would be a fluid fight without fixed lines and there would be enemy breakthroughs. Consequently the artillery had to be ready to fire in many directions. Training that stressed this ability, particularly in airborne and armor forces, paid dividends in Vietnam when the artillery found itself firing at targets in a 360-degree circle around each battery.

When Crittenberger received the order to take the

FIRE SUPPORT BASE DESIGN

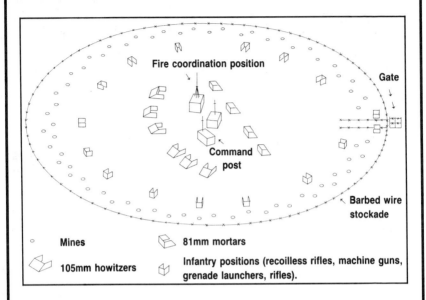

○ Mines	81mm mortars
105mm howitzers	Infantry positions (recoilless rifles, machine guns, grenade launchers, rifles).

FIRE SUPPORT BASES (FSBs) ranged from small forts sheltering just two guns to much larger, more extensive FSBs housing entire artillery battalions. Regardless of size, each FSB was designed for defense in depth and was capable of offensive fire in a 360-degree circle.

At a base's center stood a sandbag-protected observation tower. Nearby was the command post, linked by an extensive and sophisticated radio network with other FSBs in the area.

The artillery pieces stood in individual firing places bulldozed from the earth. Space permitting, these pits were positioned in order to optimize shell fire. A battery's shell pattern broke on a distant target in the same manner the guns were configured on the ground within the FSB.

The main defensive line outside these pits consisted of bunkers, foxholes, and trenches stretching in a circle around the base, defended by infantry, and linked together by concertina wire. Claymore mines and trip flares dotted the landscape close to the wire. Further out, 100 to 150 yards away, likely enemy assembly areas were strewn with bangalore torpedos and white phosphorus mines.

corps artillery to Vietnam, the II Field Force existed only on paper. Yet in a remarkable display of organizational skill and mobility, 57 days later the headquarters was in Vietnam controlling three artillery battalions engaged in combat. The force eventually grew to 13 battalions before stabilizing at a strength of 10 battalions.

All in all General Crittenberger commanded a formidable collection of 105mm and 155mm towed and self-propelled and 175mm and 8-inch self-propelled weapons. In addition four batteries of anti aircraft artillery were available both for defending fixed positions or entering the field to use their rapid-fire weapons in a direct fire role. The main factors constraining II Field Force were a lack of helicopters (in spite of the tremendous numbers of helicopters in Vietnam, everyone always wanted more) and a limited road net. Most of the II Field Force artillery were self-propelled. This meant that they were highly mobile as long as there were roads to travel on. Units operating in trackless jungle generally had to rely upon the lighter weapons of the divisional artillery. Similarly, the swampy terrain of the Mekong Delta greatly restricted the use of self-propelled weapons. The general spent his day either attending planning meetings, performing administrative paperwork, or visiting his men in the field. Planning involved figuring out how best to support future military operations. Ground combat leaders always tried to operate within range of at least one and preferably two fire support bases. In this way they maneuvered under a friendly artillery umbrella.

When a new operation was planned, the commanders asked Crittenberger whether there would be available artillery. If there wasn't the general had to establish new fire support bases. Thus a major sweep often began with helicopters delivering an infantry security team and an engineering detachment to an isolated height where the jungle would be bulldozed back to create a clearing for the artillery. One of Crittenberger's jobs was to make sure this work was done in time to support the planned sweep. Early in the war a great deal of effort went into carving out new bases. As the war progressed enough clearings were created to enable old bases to be used again.

Once the guns were in position the general oversaw

Insignia of II Field Force —The unit was assembled from scratch in 57 days, and provided the US high command with a mobile artillery force capable of being deployed throughout South Vietnam.

Brig. Gen. Willis D. Crittenberger inspecting a helicopter ammunition feed system with Army aviation weapons experts. Helicopter gunships were under Field Artillery control, and represented one of the major areas of technical innovation in the Vietnam War.

the development of a fire support scheme that would help the ground forces accomplish their mission. If helicopter assaults were planned, artillery needed to be available to deliver an initial bombardment on the landing zone. Such fire eliminated many of the mines and booby traps that otherwise ensnarled the assault infantry while driving off any defenders who planned to ambush the choppers. The long-range 175mm gun, capable of firing a 174-pound shell almost 20 miles, was the best choice for this mission. Although this weapon lacked the accuracy and jungle-penetrating power of other artillery, it was ideal for bombarding cleared landing zones.

The enemy well knew the range of the various American weapons and that ground forces were most likely to operate within this range. Since the creation of a fire support base could tip the enemy off about an impending mission, Crittenberger liked to occasionally make false moves and build fake fire support bases as a tactic of deception. A convoy of self-propelled artillery sent in the opposite direction of a planned operation or the establishment of a new base at some distance from the area of actual operations served this purpose.

Once the preparatory bombardment ended and the operation began, the commander had to rely on his subordinates' judgment to see the plan through. During this phase the general liked to visit his batteries. Arriving by helicopter on a surprise inspection he looked for several indicators of a battery's morale and efficiency. Did the men seem confident, were they smiling or sullen, would they communicate in terse monosyllables or would they talk more openly? He'd ask a soldier when had he last eaten a hot meal, taken a bath, washed his socks, received his mail. Having gotten some idea of the unit's morale the general turned his attention to its efficiency. Was the base's sanitation good or was garbage strewn about? An officer who permitted the latter condition might not be taking good care of his men. Where were the spent brass cartridges kept? In the heat of action they would be cast in any convenient direction but once the combat ended they should be picked up and stored for delivery back to base for recycling. Was the ammunition kept in a secure, dry, yet accessible place?

Crittenberger concluded his inspection with a

The view from above

SPENT CASES:
During the heat of battle nobody had time to pick up spent cartridge cases. But in the lulls in between, the generals expected their gunners to keep their gun pits clean and tidy with everything squared away.

The area of Operation Junction City —At the heart of it was FSB Gold. Junction City was the first of the big US sweep operations designed to clear the area close to the Cambodian border known as War Zone C. Beginning in February 1967 and lasting just under a month, it involved 22 US and 4 ARVN battalions and resulted in nearly 2,300 enemy killed or captured.

firing drill. He'd call out fire instructions and observe the men's actions. He secretly delighted to see the young men's reactions as they realized the old general knew their business as well as they did. Half way through the mission he ordered the men to fall out. Then he examined the levelling bubbles to see if they were properly set and verified that the gun was pointed at the aiming stake. If a battery came up short in any area he reported this fact to the divisional commander. Seldom did he have to make such a report twice.

Sometimes infantry generals relieved officers on the spot during a field inspection. This occurred when a general felt that the officers were not equal to the rigorous test of combat. These artillery officers served in a less pressured situation. Thus, their mistakes were not so severely penalized. Crittenberger never found the need to relieve an officer based on one of his inspections.

After a day in the field the general returned to headquarters. Perhaps that night he would stay up to chat with his staff, to talk shop, to try again to figure out how best to use his powerful artillery against the elusive enemy.

In the early spring of 1967, hours of meetings, careful planning, and preparation came to a climax out in a jungle clearing 55 miles northwest of Saigon.

American helicopters descended toward a blighted, tear-shaped opening in the forest. Chemical defoliants had partially created this clearing and planners intended to use it for a new fire support base, to be known as Fire Support Base Gold. This base would support a major operation called Junction City that was designed to clear the notorious War Zone C. The fire base would be smack in the middle of this war zone. However, heavy enemy contact was not expected.

Just as the first helicopters landed five tremendous explosions rocked the small clearing. Like crippled insects three choppers plummeted to the ground while six others limped away badly damaged. Anticipating an American landing, the Viet Cong had rigged heavy explosive charges and triggered them when the helicopters were at their most vulnerable.

When the smoke cleared 15 American soldiers

were dead and 28 more wounded. It was an evil beginning.

Nonetheless, helicopters continued to ferry the men of the 3d Battalion, 22d Infantry into the landing zone. Soon the men and equipment of the 2d Battalion, 77th Artillery joined them. The work of building a position for the guns began. For the entire next day the soldiers prepared their defensive positions. Worries about the terrible landing faded. Perhaps there would be no more heavy contact.

Shortly before dawn on the second morning, 20 March 1967, a patrol operating outside the defensive perimeter reported movement. Everyone tensed in anticipation of some kind of combat. Minutes ticked by slowly and nothing happened. Apparently it was a false alarm caused by some tired, jumpy infantry.

Lt. Col. John Vessey, Jr., —led the defense of FSB Gold. He later became chairman of the Joint Chiefs of Staff.

Two hours later a heavy mortar barrage crashed into the American position. Simultaneously the patrol outside the perimeter reported they were under attack. A massed enemy assault overwhelmed the patrol killing or wounding most of its men. The men inside the perimeter could not worry about the patrol's fate; they were fighting for their own lives.

Hard on the heels of the mortar bombardment, the enemy opened fire with machine guns and recoilless rifles. Their bullets and shells ranged back and forth across the perimeter.

Any damage caused by this bombardment was a bonus for the VC. Its main purpose was to force the Americans to shelter; a defender hunkered down in his foxhole could not see or use his weapon effectively. Just as American artillery tried to suppress the enemy's fire during an ambush, so the VC/NVA used their heaviest weapons—mortars, rockets, and recoilless rifles—to suppress the American fire. Once the intense bombardment had served its purpose the enemy would send in waves of attacking soldiers.

From inside the perimeter, the artillery battalion commander Lieutenant Colonel John Vessey, Jr., organized his defense. In spite of the stunning bombardment his artillerymen worked fast to return the enemy fire. Initially the enemy shelling seemed the biggest threat, so the artillery fired back at the sites where the mortars might be located. Priorities changed when the defending American infantry of

The view from above

LONG ARM:

The long range 175mm gun was the key to establishing a network of firebases, and was one of the most important weapons in the artillery arsenal. The gun's relative lack of accuracy was unimportant when it was used for its proper purpose, in preparatory bombardments for establishing bases where the enemy least expected, or least desired them.

Digging in —Grunts of the 4th Infantry Division filling sandbags near Ban Me Thout. Building extensive bases has long been an American specialty, but when you can expect to be under fire in the bunker you are digging, the quality of work goes up.

B Company radioed to Vessey's headquarters near the middle of the perimeter that Viet Cong soldiers had penetrated their lines and that they needed help fast.

Leaving their guns, the men of the 77th Artillery grabbed rifles and grenades and counterattacked the enemy breakthrough. They fought their way to the frontline defensive positions where they joined the infantry who were facing repeated VC assaults. Within half an hour of the first shelling, a forward air controller arrived overhead to coordinate air strikes against the Viet Cong. Simultaneously two batteries of 105mm howitzers positioned at nearby bases began shelling the enemy. The careful planning that positioned fire support bases in locations where they could help one another was paying off. Soon the frontline defenders called for the howitzer shells to fall just 100 meters in front of their positions. Such perilously close support was necessary because the brave enemy infantry were pressing their attacks right into point-blank range of the defenders. The artillerymen bore-sighted their pieces by squinting along the depressed gun tubes or actually looking through the open breech and out the muzzle. No fancy fire direction calculations were needed. The enemy was that close. Like waves eating away at a sand beach, successive VC assaults lapped closer and closer to the American position.

Infantry platoons from several places around the perimeter reported they were being overrun by human wave attacks. Air strikes came in terribly close to the American lines but even these failed to stem the flow. The forward air controller's plane crashed after being hit by enemy antiaircraft fire. At this desperate juncture an infantry leader called to the artillery to ask for "beehive" rounds—containers filled with hundreds of metal darts—directly into his position. The gunners responded by sending these massive shotgun-like rounds screaming through the American position. They hoped the friendlies would be protected by their dug-in positions while the exposed enemy would be hit.

Six minutes later the same American commander reported that a new enemy attack had broken through and that his men were running out of ammunition. The dwindling American infantry reserve, just 20 men, attacked toward them in order to deliver more ammunition. A quarter of an hour of hellish combat ensued and then the artillery received a report that another section of the perimeter had been overrun.

Enemy rockets had knocked out the crew of one of the quad .50 machine guns sited to defend FSB Gold. Without this weapon the Americans could not hold. As the infantry fell back the VC swarmed around the quad .50, turning it to face the remaining defenders. Seventy-five yards away an American 105mm howitzer crew calmly depressed the weapon's barrel. In the nick of time their first shot destroyed the overrun weapon.

A little over two hours into the fight half the American defenders had been pushed back from their initial positions into a final defensive perimeter. This allowed the Viet Cong to infiltrate right into the heart of FSB Gold. Soon enemy grenadiers were lobbing their deadly explosives into the command post and aid station from just five yards away. Throughout the perimeter furious hand-to-hand combat was going on as the defenders used whatever weapons they could lay their hands on

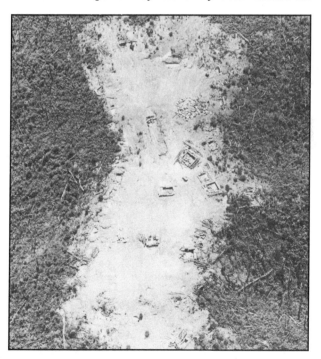

GHOST BASE: Aerial view of an abandoned FSB in the A Shau valley. Formerly home to a battery of the 101st Airborne Division, it had been picked bare before being abandoned. US troops knew that whatever they left behind would be salvaged by an enemy much-practiced in living off the land. To the NVA everything had a use; even old C-ration cans were recycled to make casings for homemade mines and grenades.

including shovels, chain saws, and bowie knives. The American artillerymen fought for their lives.

Colonel Vessey and his staff helped man the howitzers, firing beehive rounds over open sights against the enemy who stood at the impossibly close ranges of 15 to 50 meters. In a combat that would have seemed more appropriate at the Battle of Waterloo than in a war fought in high-tech modern society, the gunners fired pointblank canister into the faces of an enemy who refused to yield. Each

The view from above

CROSS COUNTRY: An 8-inch self-propelled howitzer on its way across the Song Ba River not far from Tuy Hoa. The M-107 was not supposed to ford streams more than 2½ feet deep. Here there is clearly some speculation among the local peasants and US personnel as to whether the gun will make it. It did. Tracked vehicles in the background are M-548 cargo carriers, essential for logistics in rough terrain.

beehive container sent 8,000 flechettes (finned missiles) tearing into the enemy ranks.

The supply of beehive rounds was exhausted. Still the Viet Cong attacked. The gunners switched to high explosive shells set with a minimum fuse. The shells exploded at almost the instant they left the howitzer barrel. From outside the perimeter, supporting artillery and jet aircraft blasted enemy positions. Incredible precision under stress was required as the jets and artillery dropped their

Insignia of the 77th Field Artillery —During the defense of FSB Gold, the unit fired more than 1,000 rounds against infiltrating Viet Cong forces.

ordnance within 50 meters of the American foxholes. Nonetheless the American position continued to shrink. Two and one-half hours after the fight began a relief column reached FSB Gold. They counterattacked to restore the original defensive position. Joining them came the surviving infantry of Company B, many of whom wore bandages from earlier wounds and some so badly injured that they were carried piggyback by their comrades as they advanced. Yet the Viet Cong continued to press their attacks.

Twelve minutes later American armor arrived to finally break the back of the enemy assault. The tanks literally overran the Viet Cong positions, sending the enemy survivors fleeing with a hail of machine gun and canister fire.

The combat at FSB Gold had been unusual in many ways. Few enemy units attempted to stay and fight with the Americans during daylight. Yet this enemy force had exchanged heavy blows with the defenders for some 150 minutes in spite of a withering American aerial bombardment and shelling from nearby artillery. Even the arrival of American reinforcements had failed to halt the Viet Cong. During this fight the 2d Battalion, 77th Field Artillery fired more than 1,000 rounds including 30 beehives. This was the largest number of beehive rounds fired in a single engagement to date and indicated the intensity of the close combat.

In the end the infantry's valor, coupled with the determination of the artillerymen, prevailed. It hadn't been easy or cheap; 31 Americans died and 109 were wounded. By their sacrifice FSB Gold held. In the Vietnam War, this remarkable combat came closest to seeing an American-defended fire support base overwhelmed by enemy attack.

The units and those who led them in the defense of FSB Gold went on to gain greater renown during the course of the war. The artillery battalion commander, Colonel Vessey, who survived his stint as a common gunner during the bloody March dawn, went on to become the first artilleryman to serve as chairman of the Joint Chiefs of Staff.

The involvement of artillerymen fighting alongside infantrymen at FSB Gold was unusual. Back at II Field Force headquarters, the artillery officers continued to grow frustrated. For the

majority of the time the big guns of the corps artillery fired harassment and interdiction (H&I) missions. The targets came from Vietnamese intelligence based on information gained from spies and prisoner interrogations. There was no way to assess the validity of this intelligence. Only after the war ended would America learn how completely compromised this intelligence was. The South Vietnamese Army was riddled with enemy agents. Often the enemy knew about a planned operation before the Allied units who were to participate knew. However, at the time the II Field Force made the best possible use of the resources at hand.

At least one officer wondered how the Army could win. Colonel George Allin spent hundreds of hours flying over the countryside visiting American and Allied bases. He recalled how aircraft served as the eyes of the artillerymen in earlier wars. In this war, although he did a great deal of looking, not once did he see any live enemy soldiers nor any recognizable

HEAVYWEIGHT:
The M-109 was designed to survive in the massive bombardments of a European war, but its armor and firepower, augmented by a .50-cal on the turret roof, made it an effective weapon in Vietnam, particularly in a direct fire role for perimeter defense.

The view from above

UNDER ARMOR:
Inside an M-109. Half tank and half gun, the M-109 had a crew of six, three handling ammunition. The most widely used self-propelled howitzer in the world, it has a fume extractor to keep the firing compartment clear of smoke, but it can be unpleasantly hot even with the turret hatches open.

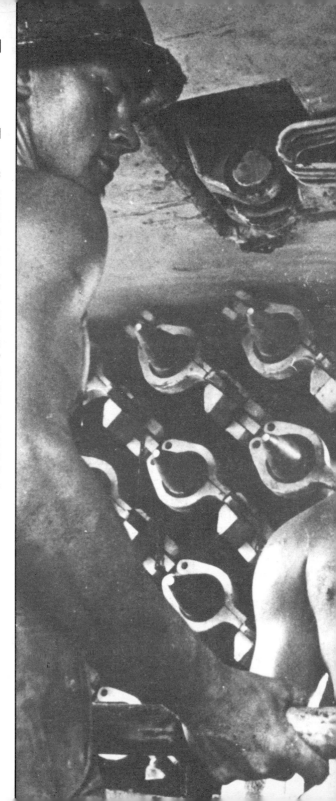

Gen. William C. Westmoreland —US commander in South Vietnam. A lifelong artilleryman, he had experience dating from the era of horse-drawn guns to the high-tech battlefield he helped to create. He paid special attention to the role of artillery in Vietnam, and was the moving spirit behind the notion of interlocking FSBs.

enemy installations. The colonel knew the simple fact was that the corps' big guns couldn't contribute if there was nothing to shoot at. He and other World War II veterans longed for the days when American artillery helped defeat repeated German tank attacks in Normandy or paved the way for the capture of the vital town of St. Lo, thus permitting the Americans to break free and sweep all the way to the German border.

Instead here in II Field Force the corps artillery played a static role. From month to month and year to year little changed. Some batteries moved from one base to another but mostly they stayed inside fixed positions. Sometimes Colonel Allin wondered why more batteries of the big 175mm guns were sent to Vietnam. There simply were not enough large and clearly defined targets for these weapons.

The commander of II Field Force, Lieutenant General Bruce Palmer, quizzed Colonel Allin, then acting commander of the II Field Force Artillery, as to exactly what purpose the corps artillery was serving. Firing H&I missions, replied Allin. Palmer doubted the value of such fire. Allin could only respond by saying there was nothing else for the guns to do. He knew Palmer's skepticism was shared by many, including officers in the artillery. The corps artillery possessed immense firepower, it was well trained and eager to help. It was simply a case of the means not matching the mission.

Faced with such frustration, planners from Westmoreland on down redoubled their efforts. Officers toiled long hours to devise a scheme to trap the enemy and force him into combat. Westmoreland visited II Field Force, explained his plan, and everyone went away impressed with how hard the general was trying. Yet after days of labor, numerous meetings, and large-scale movements of men and guns, the sweep would begin and find that the trap closed on mostly empty real estate. After supporting several such operations, Allin wondered how America was going to win this war. It seemed to him that the Army was engaged in a great deal of "thrashing around" to very little purpose.

The higher ranking officers in the 1st Infantry Division's artillery (Div Arty) tended not to share the skepticism of the corps artillerymen. They were too caught up in day-to-day action to worry about

The view from above

ORGANIZED CHAOS: Firebase Victory, just 12 miles south of the DMZ. Abandoned equipment in the water-filled crater shows the difficulty of maintaining a battery in the monsoon season. When the Americans pulled out the Viet Cong were able to glean a rich harvest of useful material that had been discarded as worthless.

The view from above

SPLIT BATTERY:
There was little demand for massive barrages by 175mm guns in Vietnam, for artillery commanders deployed smaller and more widely available weapons like 105mm and 155mm howitzers to cover contingencies like attacks on firebases. So heavy batteries were often split into three two-gun units, then combined with similar detachments of 8-inch howitzers to make up three mixed batteries of four guns each.

the broader picture. This was particularly true for the commander of all the division's artillery; the lean, aggressive General Larry Caruthers.

In the course of a year the division artillery fired close to 2.5 million rounds. A frequent and common mission was landing zone preparation. Every available piece of artillery would be used to prepare and clear the landing zone until it was safe enough for the helicopters to deliver the infantry without opposition.

The process of clearing a landing zone called for skilled coordination. It began with ten minutes of fire, carefully orchestrated by forward observers flying over the target in light observation aircraft. The best observers could handle five batteries at a time.

They directed the artillery to move around the perimeter to strike all possible enemy positions. One minute after the last shell landed the helicopters arrived. As the infantry moved out from the LZ, the forward observers requested periodic registration shots fired at known locations on the map. The infantry then marched toward the impact point. In heavily wooded terrain it was the only way they could keep from getting lost. The registration shots served a second purpose: should the infantry become engaged, the FO had a known reference point from which to adjust fires for defense of his own unit.

In addition to LZ preparation, every few months major truck convoys were dispatched to resupply fire support bases. Caruthers had his batteries line the

Brig. Gen. Lawrence H. Caruthers —commander of the 1st Infantry Division artillery. He successfully bet a case of beer on the ability of his 8-inch howitzers to score direct hits on an enemy rice cache.

entire road so that the convoy had fire support during the entire trip. A combination of self-propelled guns stationed along the road and towed artillery flown into FSBs provided total coverage. To coordinate all this artillery, aerial observers flew overhead, watching as the convoy churned along Route 13.

A particular trouble spot for the division was "The Dutchman's"—a plantation area bordering Route 13. In addition to being adjacent to the American supply route, The Dutchman's was a critical point in a major NVA supply network. The division decided to position some artillery squarely athwart the enemy trail. Caruthers favored such aggressive artillery placement. He conceived of the artillery as baiting the enemy, with the guns being the cheese in the mousetrap. At The Dutchman's it worked. That night the enemy attacked and suffered a terrible drubbing from point-blank artillery fire.

After one such successful "baiting" operation, General Caruthers visited the victorious artillerymen. The scene presented a typical picture of the artillery in Vietnam. Around each gun position lay heaps of shell casings and unexpended powder piled four feet deep. Tired gunners, many stripped to the waist, others wearing torn, sweat-soaked fatigues, leaned against the sandbags.

Caruthers ordered the men to clean the position up. He worried that all the unused powder presented an explosive hazard. A badly fatigued section chief responded. He picked up an empty shell casing that was perforated with bullet holes and began filling it with discarded powder.

"Get with it" the section chief ordered his men.

The general interrupted: "Put that thing out."

The section chief was dragging on a cigarette as he handled the loose powder. After the dangers of close-range night combat, the risk of self-immolation from a burning ember seemed trivial.

As a disciplinarian he felt that two mistakes could be understood, a third was grounds for dismissal. One hard-headed battalion commander seemed not to take advice well. One day as helicopters were minutes away from a landing zone that the artillery was supposed to prepare, Caruthers learned that no shells were breaking on the target. The battalion commander had made a serious mistake. His guns

were shelling the wrong LZ! He was relieved from command.

Making sure the artillery officers were top-rate mattered in critical situations. On one occasion the 1st Division infantry had walked into an L-shaped ambush. A terrific fight ensued. The FO called for help. The 1/33 Artillery was on an airstrip about 4,000 meters away. The FO was popping smoke into which the artillery was firing. An air observer watched with alarm and entered the radio net:

"The artillery is breaking right in the smoke. That's where our guys are!"

"It's all right," responded the FO, "it's breaking right where we need it, that's where the NVA are." The enemy was using hugging tactics, trying to fight inside of the artillery support, but the Americans weren't responding as expected. Instead they just called the artillery in closer.

The 1/33 was firing at the rate of about 5,000 rounds per hour. This would quickly exceed the

ON TARGET: Infantrymen welcomed the support this 8-inch howitzer could give. Spacing between the guns was reduced from the ideal 100 meters to 35-50 meters to keep the perimeters defensible. Note the crew using their hands rather than earmuffs to deafen the noise.

The view from above

DEFENSIVE FIRE: An M-102 working hard to repulse an attack on a 101st Airborne Division firebase. The high rate of fire of the M-102, up to ten rounds per minute, and the ease with which its lightweight carriage could swivel to face a surprise attack made it one of the most effective close range weapons firing either beehive, Improved Conventional Munitions, or ''Killer Junior'' preset fuzes on high explosive rounds.

The view from above

GRENADE-LOADED:
Improved Conventional Munition (ICM) rounds, first used in 1968, were considered more effective as anti-personnel weapons than beehive rounds where the enemy infantry were lying down or crawling. A 155mm ICM round contained 60 grenades, known as ''sub-munitions.'' They were pushed out of the shell base by an expelling charge. As they fell, small guiding vanes opened so that the striker plate hit the ground first, detonating a small charge that threw a steel ball full of explosive, scattering shrapnel over the target area.

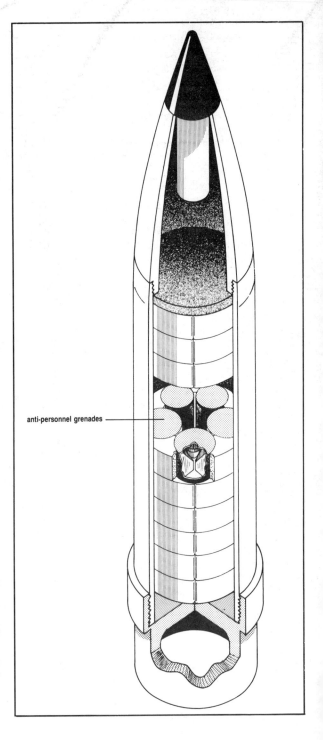

anti-personnel grenades

available supply. Caruthers heard this and ordered the ready artillery ammunition, 100 bags previously prepared as a reserve, sent to the fast-firing guns. "Hooks," C-47 helicopters, starting flying it in. Meanwhile the Air Force delivered more ammunition on C-123s to an airbase near the artillery depot. Infantrymen assigned perimeter defense carried it to the Hooks.

With an uninterrupted flow of ammunition, the guns continued to fire. The actuator handles broke off from the overstressed weapons. The crew substituted screwdrivers set directly into the breech. The paint on the gun tubes blistered from the heat generated by the rapid fire.

But the artillerymen's support was successful. Deadly airbursts splintered the jungle, sending a lethal rain of wood and metal fragments tearing into human flesh. The jungle was reduced to matchwood with nothing over knee height remaining. The ground was littered with pieces of wood and chunks of human flesh, the remnants of the NVA attackers.

Occasionally the divisional artillery fired at enemy installations or base camps.

One time Caruthers received a call: "Hey, we have a rice cache out here. It's too far out to carry back and with darkness approaching there's no time to bring choppers in. What do you recommend to destroy it?"

"I'll use 8-inch howitzers," Caruthers replied.

"Bet you won't hit it."

"All right, that's a case of beer," answered the general.

He called the battery, provided target data, and observed with satisfaction as the fifth round hit the rice cache.

The artillery fire was interrupted by a new message: "I've got three navy bombers here, and if I don't use them they will go away."

Accordingly, the artillery suspended fire while the bombers dropped their ordnance all around the target, but failed to score a direct hit.

Amused, General Caruthers ordered the 8-inch artillery to resume firing. He knew they were the most accurate weapon in the American arsenal. The artillery completed the job and the general collected his case of beer.

Ready-frozen —Loaders freeze (arm) the detonator fuzes onto an 8-inch howitzer in readiness for a fire mission. The 8-inch had the sort of accuracy generals made bets about.

Artillery vs. artillery

9

The battle for Khe Sanh

IT WAS AN ARTICLE of faith among American military leaders that whichever side gained fire superiority would win the battle. The officers of Colonel David Lownds's 26th Marines believed that their isolated post at Khe Sanh depended on fire superiority to survive. Although aircraft could deliver an awesome amount of deadly ordnance, air operations could be hampered by weather conditions. Frequently Khe Sanh lay blanketed by fog and low-hanging clouds. Thus, as the so-called siege of Khe Sanh began, Colonel Lownds remarked that the side that kept its artillery intact would win. At the outset it was not entirely clear that the Americans would be that side.

The 77-day battle of Khe Sanh marked the most intense duel between American and North Vietnamese artillery during the Vietnam War. The enemy labored mightily to gain artillery superiority. In this effort they were greatly aided by geography. Khe Sanh lay on top of a small plateau. Surrounding and overshadowing it were numerous piedmont hills with jungle slopes topped by tall tropical hardwoods. To defend the base the Marines had to defend certain nearby key hills. Whoever controlled this high ground controlled Khe Sanh. Consequently it was no secret to the North Vietnamese where the American defenders would be.

To get at them the NVA forces utilized two artificial barriers: the demilitarized zone separating North from South Vietnam and the nearby Laotian border. Behind these lines they massed men and material, knowing they were secure from American attack. But to attack Khe Sanh directly they had to cross trackless, mountainous jungle while under ferocious bombardment from American aircraft. The

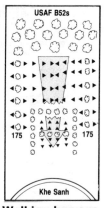

Walking barrage —Elaborate artillery barrages were used to break up massive NVA infantry attacks on Khe Sanh. Three batteries inside the base aimed to isolate the lead battalion in the assault, while the fourth "walked" a barrage from one end of the "box" to the other. Simultaneously, the fire support coordination center used 175mm guns from neighboring bases to make two sides of a wider box around the second and third waves of attackers.

movement of forces began. As American intelligence identified regiment after regiment of regular North Vietnamese soldiers, including famous units that had participated in the capture of Dien Bien Phu, everyone up to and including President Johnson grew worried. The situation looked bleak.

The campaign began in February 1966, when Army heavy artillery at the Con Thien Marine Fire Base initiated a heavy bombardment of suspected enemy positions. The next day the enemy responded with a series of rocket and artillery attacks against American positions. A prolonged artillery duel ensued lasting many days. The terrific exchange of heavy ordnance drove both the Americans and the North Vietnamese underground. Only by digging deeply could anyone on either side survive the bombardment. In time the trees surrounding American strongpoints along the hills became so riddled with shrapnel fragments that the engineers' efforts to cut them down only resulted in ruined chain saw blades. The Marine position with its deep entrenchments and underground bunkers, its surface pummeled into a cratered moonscape by the constant artillery bombardment, resembled nothing so much as the Western Front in World War I.

In spite of the enemy's bombardment, the Marine artillery remained intact. Each gun lay safely tucked away inside heavily sandbagged fortifications. Although the crews were often showered by shrapnel, only a direct hit squarely on top could knock a gun out. This seldom happened. Sheltered from enemy bombardment, the Marine artillery roared back in defiance. During the 77-day battle, it answered each enemy round with ten of its own. This was fire superiority.

The defense of Khe Sanh did not rely purely on artillery housed within its perimeter. In addition to some 40 pieces at Khe Sanh, there were sixteen 175mm Army pieces sited at nearby bases, like Camp Carroll, from which they could be fired in support of Khe Sanh. With so much firepower at hand, the Marines utilized a level of massed battery fire rarely employed at any other point during the war. These fires included time-on-target (TOT) bombardments where numerous batteries synchronized their shells' fuzes and staggered their time of firing so that all exploded simultaneously; artillery boxes—

Following the Soviet tradition, the NVA and Viet Cong used rockets extensively as effective lightweight artillery with considerable destructive power. These captured 122mm rounds were set up to show a visiting VIP the three basic launch methods. They look crude, but when the target is a large firebase like Khe Sanh, more elaborate and accurate, methods are unnecessary and may simply lead to the firer's early detection.

squares on a map—where the shells boxed in a designated area so no one could escape while high explosives pelted the box's interior; and rolling barrages where the shells marched steadily forward along the ground obliterating everything in their path.

In the words of the Marines' target intelligence officer, "an average night's pattern of pre-planned fires was. . . combined TOTs from nine batteries; separate battalion TOTs; battery multiple volley individual missions; battery H&Is." As long as Khe Sanh received supplies, the defending artillery could put up a steel curtain around the grunts huddled deep inside their bunkers. Eventually, the artillery accumulated more ammunition than it could store. Part of this excess was some 90 rounds of green smoke. On St. Patrick's Day the Marine gunners deluged enemy positions with the smoke to honor the patron saint of the fighting Irish. The Marine gunners also worked hard at quickly responding to calls for fire. Periodically Colonel Lownds visited the Fire Direction Center, pointed to a location on the map, and ordered the gunners to hit it. On average a shell left a barrel aimed toward this target within

MARKER SHELL:
Artillerymen at
Khe Sanh watch
white
phosphorus
shells landing
just outside the
perimeter. Most
attacks took
place at night.

40 seconds. Faced with such extraordinary firepower, the North Vietnamese could and did hit back. An average of 150 rounds of mortar, rocket, and artillery fire fell within the base each day. During one peak day in February, over 1,300 rounds blasted Khe Sanh. The North Vietnamese exhibited cool, professional judgment in their artillery tactics. The 122mm rocket was a favorite weapon. This Soviet-made rocket was accurate in a left and right direction but was erratic on distance. Accordingly,

the NVA sited their rockets so they tracked along Khe Sanh's long axis. In that way any shorts or longs still landed within the perimeter. About 5,000 122mm rockets landed inside Khe Sanh during the extended battle.

The heaviest of the NVA artillery was sited 20 miles away in the Cam Roc mountain across the Laotian border. Skillfully camouflaged, the 130mm and 152mm batteries proved exceptionally difficult for the Americans to locate. Not only were they well

Moment of impact —An ammunition bunker at Khe Sanh combat base explodes after it is hit by an enemy rocket in the attack of January 21, 1968, at the start of the 77-day siege. The loss of 1,500 tons of bombs, shells, mines, and bullets without the prospect of immediate resupply kept the Marine artillery severely rationed.

hidden, but NVA gunners usually fired only a few rounds per hour so that constant muzzle flashes would not reveal their location. After firing, the guns were run back inside their concealed and protected positions, often inside caves hollowed out of the surrounding hills. The big shells proved deadly effective. Even a dud would penetrate the Khe Sanh runway—the base's lifeline—to a depth of four feet.

Eventually some of the big guns were silenced thanks to the phenomenal patience and eagle-eyed observation of a Molikau Niuatoa, an American-Samoan Marine who had scored 241 in marksmanship in boot camp.

Based on Hill 881S, one of the hills that guarded Khe Sanh, Niuatoa had been assigned to look west to the Laotian border to see if he could figure out where the enemy artillery was based. Armed with 20-power binoculars he would pick a likely spot and freeze his eyes on it and watch until the artillery fired. If he did not detect anything in the area he was looking at when the artillery fired, he would move his binoculars a fraction and watch another spot until the artillery fired. This process of elimination, staring 10 or more miles into the distance for up to 14 hours a day, lasted 30 days before Niuatoa thought he had spotted something. The big Samoan—call sign "Pineapple Chunk"—had spotted a pinpoint of light. Every time he saw it, there was the sound, 15 to 20 seconds later, of a gun going off.

A flight of four A-4 Skyhawks was called in. They dropped a stick of bombs onto a ridge some 15 kilometers away and Niuatoa used this as his reference point for directing them on target. His first instruction was: "Left one click (kilometer), add two ridge lines." His next instruction was "Drop about halfway down the ridgeline and come left about 500 meters." Another stick of bombs moved closer to the target. After two more adjustments the bombs created a massive hole, blowing away a large bamboo camouflage mat to reveal a 130mm gun. More bombs destroyed it and over the next few days A-4s worked their way along the ridgeline destroying four more enemy guns.

THOSE WHO SURVIVED at Khe Sanh quickly became attuned to the sound of incoming enemy fire. They could tell in an instant whether the whistling

noise overhead was coming at them or about to hit some other part of the base. The almost apocryphal story is told of a group of Marines on leave from Khe Sanh at the big Marine base at Da Nang. While they are watching the movie *One Million Years B.C.*, a distant voice yelled "Incoming!"

As shells began to explode the screen faded. Most of the crowd and the projectionist ran for bunkers. But not the Khe Sanh vets, who'd recognized the sound of mortar fire falling short of their position. Instead they turned on the projectionist. One Khe Sanh vet threatened by shouting: "Turn that thing back on or I'll blow you away." As more enemy rockets and mortars landed the vets restarted the projector. Another distant voice yelled: "They're infiltrating!" The movie viewers opened fire all around the perimeter of the makeshift theater. Their fire served as a warning to all comers. "Everybody knew not to come in there while we were watching the film," one grunt explained.

A Marine replacement who arrived during the

CLOSE RANGE:
Marine gun batteries inside Khe Sanh were assigned the targets that came naturally—the first wave of attackers—while the more complex and less directly effective bombardment of NVA support positions was left to long range guns from other bases and the Air Force.

height of the artillery duel at Khe Sanh recalls his fear when he was told that he was to go out on patrol.

He had only arrived a few hours ago and now he had to venture out into the unknown. Leaving the protective wire he and his patrol marched a few hundred meters. Behind them came the sound of multiple explosions. One of the veterans, a haggard,

Artillery vs. artillery

MORTAR TEAM: The mortars were the last layer of the artillery defense of Khe Sanh. Their relatively small lethal burst meant they could be used on attackers right up to the wire. Before opening fire (inset left) the tube is adjusted for azimuth and range, while rounds are fuzed and stacked ready. In action a good mortar squad (center) works a rhythm that keeps a constant barrage going, taking turns to rest (inset right). With up to 1,000 rounds a day incoming, flak jackets became standard body armor.

hollow-eyed grunt, commented: "Be thankful you're out on patrol, because they're catching hell back there." "Is there incoming every day?" inquired the replacement. "Yeah, five times a day. We wake up to incoming. We have incoming for lunch. It hits again about seven in the evening and again about ten-thirty or eleven. It depends on how the NVA feels."

139

White Eyes 37

10

Short-range patrols

THEY RANGED in age from 20 to 23 years old. The five members of White Eyes 37 hailed from places like Opelika, Alabama; Sherman Oaks, California; and Memphis, Tennessee. They were common infantrymen with little special training. Sergeant Green, their 22-year-old leader, was a seasoned veteran, close to 10 months in-country. One private had been in Vietnam for a mere month. They were members of a short-range patrol code-named "White Eyes 37."

The 4th Division artillery, operating in Quang Duc Province, needed targets. One of the jobs of the short-range patrols was to find them. Their mission was "to observe for enemy activity." At noon on September 23, 1968, the five rifle-armed Americans from Company C, 2d Battalion, 35th Infantry, set off into the jungle. They marched for about an hour to the slope of a jungle-covered ridge where they deployed 15 meters away from the bend of a seemingly unused trail. The patrol could see 30 to 40 meters in both directions along the trail. Hidden in the dense vegetation they waited for three hours, silent and alone except for the buzzing of insects.

Insignia of the 35th Infantry.

Suddenly talking and laughter broke the silence. The Americans became rigidly alert. Five unwary NVA soldiers sauntered carelessly down the trail. Right in front of the hidden Americans they sat down and began to eat. Sergeant Green considered opening fire, but remembering his mission was to "observe," decided against it. After 10 minutes the NVA soldiers continued along the trail. The Americans breathed easier. A few minutes later the clanging of equipment and sounds of tromping feet again broke the silence. Filing along the trail came first 10, then 40, then a seemingly endless column of equipment-laden NVA soldiers. Luckily, the

column had no flank security, no one beating the
bush in case the Americans were present. White
Eyes 37 stayed hidden just 15 meters away from the
NVA battalion. Over two hours the patrol counted
487 enemy soldiers carrying mortars, rockets, and
machine guns. They marched quickly but seemed
relaxed. Darkness came and still the column
marched on. Enemy officers carried flashlights to
preserve order. White Eyes 37 counted another 100
enemy soldiers before there was a break in the column. Sergeant Green turned on his radio and
whispered to a forward observer what they had seen.
The FO called divisional artillery, described the
target, and provided the location.

The artillerymen raced to position their guns. Here, at last, was a real target; one with live enemy soldiers, one they could blast at with conviction; a target to make up for boring weeks spent firing blindly into the jungle. Rapidly and skillfully the gunners laid their pieces. The first smoke rounds landed 25 to 50 meters in front of White Eyes 37. As the shells landed the NVA reacted immediately. They knew what was about to happen. They scattered into the ravines bordering the trail as a hurricane of high explosive shells saturated the area.

The distant FO moved the artillery fire up and down the trail. To have concentrated the fire in front of White Eyes 37 would have given away the

People detector —In 1968 ADSID (Aerial Delivered Seismic Intrusion Detector) units like this, camouflaged to merge with the vegetation, were dropped by the thousands from planes flying over the Ho Chi Minh Trail, the enemy's main supply route from North to South Vietnam. An ADSID unit was sensitive enough to detect the movement of soldiers along a trail. Linked by radio to a central intelligence point, they helped provide a picture of enemy movements and reduced the need for target-seeking forays.

American position. As the shells broke Sergeant Green motioned for his men to take off their equipment. Even their dog tags were removed so they could crawl silently in the darkness. Each man grasped the legs of the man in front so they could stay together.

Around them flashlights flickered as NVA officers tried to regroup their men. The enemy were trying to crawl free of the fire zone whenever the artillery fire shifted elsewhere. When the shelling returned everyone went to cover. The crying of the enemy wounded and the sounds of excited, frightened Vietnamese voices filled the air.

White Eyes 37 moved right through the disorganized NVA battalion. At times they passed within arm's reach of prone enemy soldiers. Some spoke to them. The Americans didn't answer and crawled on. The patrol sought out the thickest vegetation 300 meters off the trail and tried to hide as best they could. There they spent an uneasy night, one interrupted by the light and noise of random American artillery shells. At first light, they saw NVA soldiers resting 10 meters away. Like the Americans these men had simply crawled away from the fire, seeking the best shelter they could find. The enemy departed without noticing them, and the shaken American patrol returned safely to base.

For the officers of the 4th Division, White Eyes 37 had been a complete success. A major enemy unit had been found and badly mauled.

The men of White Eyes 37 felt differently. When the first shells exploded just in front of them they had been certain they were about to die. Only one soldier had been hit by American shrapnel and he hadn't realized it until the next day.

Only days later could White Eyes 37 articulate what they had seen and done. They agreed that the only thing that had saved them was that each soldier had done exactly what he had needed to do. Had one man faltered the patrol would have been lost. Although proud of their performance they questioned their mission: "I don't think it's safe for five men to be out there," one complained. The complaints of privates seldom register on the ears of the high command. They believed that missions such as White Eyes 37 were what it took to find the enemy in the jungles of Vietnam.

HIGH TECH ON THE BATTLEFIELD

1st Cav Div artillerymen preparing an antipersonnel radar unit at FSB Nancy. Electronic surveillance devices like these were invaluable in providing perimeter security at semipermanent FSBs, where there were insufficient infantry.

Electronic sensors were also used aggressively in the latter years of the war. In one incident on August 29, 1970, an NVA battalion, marching along a road in Binh Dinh Province, was struck by a barrage of mortar and 105mm howitzer fire. The battalion dispersed and fled toward some nearby mountains. Artillery, mortar, and quad-.50 machine gun fire blocked all lines of retreat. Yet no enemy soldier had seen an American face.

Instead the NVA had been ''seen'' by a string of remote control sensors linked to a nearby American base. These devices had been arrayed in a series, so that they would provide as complete as possible a picture of the enemy position. Magnetic devices indicated the presence of weapons and equipment, acoustic devices picked up the sounds of Vietnamese voices, while seismic sensors detected movement.

They were just part of a host of high-tech gadgets used to find targets for the artillery; short-range radar was used for detecting troop movement, while longer range radar was deployed to track the flight of enemy shells so American artillery could accurately return fire. There were even chemical detectors called ''people sniffers.'' Under the right circumstances they worked well. But most of these devices were still in their infancy and they were seldom as accurate as the direct observation provided by flesh-and-blood US soldiers.

Prisoner of war

11

Frontline artillery

IN 1972 THE LAST American ground troops withdrew from Vietnam. The big guns of the field artillery were either transferred to the South Vietnamese Army or accompanied the artillerymen home. However, a powerful American presence remained. The artillery had taken to the air. Rocket- and machine-gun-armed Cobra helicopters continued to support ARVN ground forces. Artillery officers flew many of these powerful gunships. They struggled daily to make up for the missing firepower of the departed American artillery.

Unlike the field artillery, the aerial rocket artillery (ARA) gunners saw their targets before they fired. The ground troops would release smoke grenades to mark the friendly position. The pilot would confirm the sighting. He would then approach perpendicular to the front line, a precaution so that short or long shots would not strike friendly troops, and release his withering rocket barrage. When North Vietnam launched its massive assault in the spring of 1972 the ARA helicopter pilots were pressed to their limits.

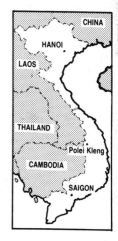

One of these pilots was Captain William Reeder, Jr. On a May morning in 1972 he prepared to lead a two-Cobra-gunship flight. His mission was to respond instantly to any tactical emergency (TAC-E) calls for help.

Just after dawn the first call came: "TAC-E! Tanks at Polei Klang."

The Cobras lifted off the ground and rushed into position to cover some special tank-killing helicopters. The target was hidden, but another message came through diverting the flight to nearby Ben Het where North Vietnamese armor was rolling over the defensive barbed wire in an overwhelming attack

147

designed to crush an ARVN unit and its American advisers.

Captain Reeder appraised the situation. Tanks and infantry pressed the defenders hard. Intense enemy antiaircraft fire swept the skies yet thick, low-hanging clouds prevented the choppers from climbing to safety. The captain sent his helicopter diving to treetop level and began his firing pass. A stream of red tracers swept past his plexiglass cockpit. Suddenly the chopper shuddered with the impact of machine gun bullets.

"This is Panther 36 taking fire three o'clock. . . taking hits, taking hits—we're going down."

Reeder awoke face down in the dirt. A horrible pain sent waves of agony up and down his back. Fighting to orient himself, the captain tried to use the emergency radio to call for help. It wouldn't work. He checked his condition. He wiped his forehead and noticed that his hand was covered in blood. His legs responded unwillingly to efforts to move. A metal fragment protruded from his foot. To remain in this position meant certain capture. Reeder began to crawl.

Briefly his mind cleared. He had been flying a Cobra, not the fixed-wing aircraft he had been shot down in years earlier. That meant he had a copilot. Where was he? Waves of pain swept over him and he lost consciousness.

He awakened to the sound of helicopters. He tried to signal. Two low-flying Cobras rapidly flew toward him. "Thank God! Rescue," he thought. The Cobras opened fire with their miniguns. Diving into the underbrush, pursued by a stream of bullets pelting the ground all around, Reeder narrowly avoided death. As the adrenaline rush subsided, he listened to the nearby sounds of helicopters hovering. At least his copilot was being rescued.

By the next morning he found he could walk short distances. Periodically during that day and the next he tried to signal to friendly aircraft. Only one saw him. Mistaking him for an enemy soldier this plane drove him into a bomb crater with machine gun fire.

Hobbling along he noted that his body seemed weak from blood loss and hunger. He relied upon his survival training: eat a small amount of something and wait. If nothing bad happens eat some more and wait. If again nothing bad happens it's edible. His

meals began to consist of leaves and ants. While eating he calculated that friendly troops lay 20 or so miles away and that he could make it in two weeks at the painfully slow rate he traveled.

A low-flying plane appeared. Firing his emergency flares the captain tried to attract its attention. Instead enemy soldiers saw him. Stumbling into the jungle Reeder went to ground near a small stream. There he waited quietly, hoping to evade detection. After a time he moved on.

On the third day his back worsened. Determined to survive he continued to walk, pausing only to pull off leeches and eat handfuls of leaves. Shouts interrupted his progress. Five NVA soldiers appeared, pointing their assault rifles at his head. With a feeling of absolute despair, Captain Reeder raised his hands. He was a prisoner of war.

The enemy soldiers took him a short distance to a concealed camp. Being frontline soldiers they treated him reasonably during the first day, merely stripping him of his possessions. All that changed with the arrival of an English-speaking interrogator. Tied to a tree he was badly beaten during the day. At night he slept in the mud.

The interrogator told him on the third day to prepare for travel. As the battered pilot left with his

Prisoner of war

guards his torturer said: "Try to make it." Three agonizing days passed, stumbling through the jungle, dodging Allied airstrikes. To falter meant death, as his guards constantly reminded him. Finally he arrived at a second camp housing one other American and some 300 South Vietnamese. Twenty-six soldiers lay with their feet confined in stocks in a tiny bamboo cage four and one-half feet high. Once a day they went to a filthy latrine.

After two months undergoing periodic interrogations, and with only a grapefruit-sized rice ball to eat each day Reeder's condition worsened. Without medical help infection worked its way into his ankle. Without adequate food he lost weight.

Then a nightmare-like march north began. Reeder was a walking skeleton, and his back pained him greatly. Dysentery further wracked his body. The

ankle infection spread until the guards threatened
to amputate it. His one American comrade died.
Vivid hallucinations mixed with pain became his
companions. Throughout, the only thing that helped
Reeder endure this unrelieved hell was a real desire
to see his copilot again, to have a drink with him,
to find out what happened. The three-month journey
ended in Hanoi. At this time the North Vietnamese
had radically changed their behavior toward POWs.
Conditions were tolerable. In the spring of 1973 the
artillery captain and other American prisoners were
released.

Arriving at a hospital in the Philippines, Reeder
learned his back had been broken and that he had
malaria as well as three kinds of worms. Worse, he
learned that his copilot had been rescued, only to
die on his way to the hospital.

Killer Jr., Killer Sr.

12

Defending FSBs

THE POLICY OF "BULLETS, not bodies" led US forces in Vietnam, especially the artillery, to fight a highly mechanized war. Where once US troops would have directly engaged the enemy in one-on-one combat, they now engaged with vast volumes of firepower.

New tactics were constantly evolved as officers in the field experimented to find the most effective way of halting an enemy attack.

One such direct fire tactic was "Killer Junior." Time-fuzed shells, fired by 105mm and 155mm artillery, were set to explode 30 feet off the ground at ranges of 200 to 1,000 meters. The shortest range fuze was intended to explode just 100 meters outside the defensive perimeter. Progressively saturating an area just outside an FSB perimeter with low-level airbursts like these created a killing zone in which no living thing could survive. The "Killer Junior" system often was more effective than beehive rounds. The attacker could duck under the 8,000 metal arrows in the beehive round and continue to advance by crawling on the ground. There was no such escape from "Killer Junior." ("Killer Senior" was the same system employed by the heavy 8-inch howitzer. The name "Killer" came from the radio call sign of the 1st Battalion, 8th Artillery, the unit that perfected the tactic.)

Using "Killer Junior/Killer Senior" tactics, and firing beehive or special rounds packed with small antipersonnel grenades known as ICMs (improved conventional munitions), gave US troops overwhelming firepower superiority. Consequently, the enemy was never able to take an American fire support base.

Over time, the VC/NVA forces learned to avoid

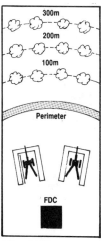

The killing zone beyond the perimeter created by the Killer Jr. tactic

attacking prepared American positions. Instead
they concentrated on attacking American units out
in the bush while they were moving. The enemy
tried to surprise unprepared units in ambushes or
while making helicopter assaults into landing
zones. Even in these situations, where the VC/NVA
held every advantage, they knew they had to strike
fast before the American artillery tilted the balance
of combat.

Killer Jr., Killer Sr.

KILLER JR.:
In the final analysis the guns that did the most damage to the enemy in Vietnam were light and medium pieces like this 105mm of the elite 173d Airborne Brigade. The 105mm was used at short range to ward off infantry attacks on the FSBs.

One American platoon leader described the overwhelming advantage of American firepower: "We could concentrate power on any enemy who chose to stay and fight it out. If an American unit could survive the first minutes of fighting, normally it could survive the battle. Consequently, the enemy attacking us was forced to face an unpleasant but simple decision: stay and die or break contact."

ARA — Aerial rocket artillery.

Arty — Artillery.

ARVN — Army of the Republic of Vietnam (South Vietnam).

Beehive — Artillery rounds filled with thousands of small metal flechettes which burst in a 30° arc.

DMZ — Demilitarized Zone. Established by the 1954 Geneva accords, provisionally dividing Vietnam along the 17th Parallel.

FDC — Fire directional center. Translates a request for fire support into data for ground artillery.

FO — Forward artillery observer.

FSB — Fire support base.

Gun, 175mm — Army weapon mounted on a tracked chassis and able to fire a 147-pound shell almost 33,000m max. Rate of fire is one round every two minutes.

H&I — Harassment and interdiction fire.

HE — High explosive.

Howitzer, 105mm — Standard light artillery piece, with a maximum range of about 11,000m and maximum fire rate of five rounds per minute.

Huey — Nickname for UH-1 series utility helicopters.

ICMs — Improved conventional munitions, containing sub-munitions.

LZ — Landing Zone. Usually a small clearing secured temporarily for the landing of resupply helicopters. Some became more permanent and eventually became base camps.

Mil — Millivadiers. The metric angular measurement used by NATO armed forces. One mil is the angle that subtends a base of one meter at one km distance. There are 6,400 mils in a circle.

Montagnard — Indigenous hill-dwelling people of Indochina.

Glossary

Mortar, 4.2-inch	— Largest of marine mortars at Khe Sanh, it has a rifled bore and can fire with effect some 4,000m. The shell has in its base a soft metal that expands into the rifling when the propellant explodes.
Mortar, 81mm	— US Army weapon capable of propelling a shell over an effective range up to 3,650m.
Mortar, 82mm	— Intermediate mortar used by the North Vietnamese with an effective range of about 3,000m.
Napalm	— Incendiary used in Vietnam by the French and the Americans as both a defoliant and antipersonnel weapon.
NVA	— North Vietnamese Army. Often used colloquially to refer to North Vietnamese soldier in the same way as "ARVN" was used to designate a South Vietnamese soldier.
POW	— Prisoner of war.
RTO	— Radio telephone operator.
Rocket, 122mm	— This North Vietnamese weapon, much used at Khe Sanh, makes up in mobility, ease of operation, and range for its lack of accuracy.
Sapper	— VC commando, usually armed with explosives.
TAC	— Tactical Air Command.
TAC-E	— Tactical emergency.
Tet	— The lunar New Year, a time of celebration throughout South Vietnam.
TOT	— Time on target bombardment.
VC	— Viet Cong.
Viet Cong	— A contraction of Vietnam Cong San (Vietnamese Communist).
Viet Minh	— Communist coalition founded by Ho Chi Minh in May 1941.
Vietnamization	— Term given to President Nixon's phased withdrawal of US troops and transfer of their responsibilities to South Vietnam.

About the author

James R. Arnold

James R. Arnold is a freelance writer who has contributed to numerous military journals and is the author of a history of the US Army Corps of Engineers' role in the Lincoln Memorial. He wrote *Armor* for the *Illustrated History of the Vietnam War* series.

A specialist on the Napoleonic campaigns, he has written on Napoleon's marshals and is writing a study of Napoleon's 1809 campaign. He is also writing a historical novel about the Civil War, centered on the Blue Ridge Mountains near Berryville, Virginia, where he lives.

Born in 1952 in Harvey, Illinois, James R. Arnold spent his formative years overseas and used the opportunity to study the sites of famous battles. Tours of Normandy and the Ardennes, coupled with a visit to Paris for Napoleon's bicentennial, prompted him to pursue historical study. Encouraged by scholars at the UK's Sandhurst Military Academy, he had his first work published in the British Journal of the Society for Army Historical Research.

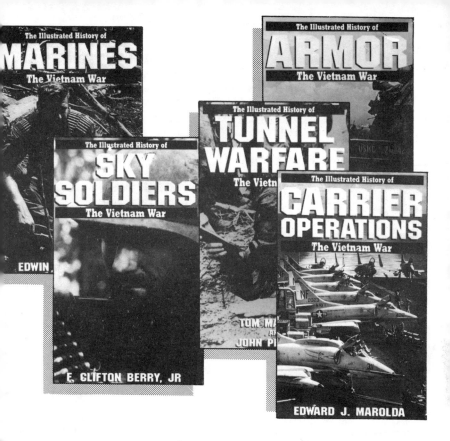

THE ILLUSTRATED
HISTORY OF
THE VIETNAM WAR

n's Illustrated History of the
m War is a unique and new
of books exploring in depth the
at seared America to the core:
that cost 58,022 American lives,
aw great heroism and re-
fulness mixed with terrible
ction and tragedy.
Illustrated History of the Viet-
/ar examines exactly what hap-
: every significant aspect—the
al details, the operations and

the strategies behind them—is analyz-
ed in short, crisply written original
books by established historians and
journalists.

Some books are devoted to key battles and campaigns, others unfold the
stories of elite groups and fighting
units, while others focus on the role
of specific weapons and tactics.

Each volume is totally original and
is richly illustrated with photographs,
line drawings, and maps.